A New Angle on Masonic Secrets

Former Worshipful Master reveals how the Lodge really works

(even Freemasons will be surprised!)

Hugh McFarland

Copyright

Table of Contents

Preface

What is it that stops a level headed businessman, who decided to give up his time-consuming hobby of Freemasonry after many years involvement including being a Worshipful Master, from divulging, even to his closest friends, any aspects about Masonic rituals and practices, even though he, and most of those he knew that were still in it, regarded them as harmless and meaningless?

This question puzzled me for a long time after I had left the "Craft". Why was I still giving evasive answers to enquirers rather than the facts? Was it out of loyalty to my ex-brethren, was it out of a fear of retribution of some kind, was it because I had taken an oath, was I simply embarrassed or was my free will affected somehow?

Then I discovered that although I had resigned from my Lodge, I hadn't actually left Freemasonry. There is no formal procedure to voluntarily resign from Freemasonry. The only Brethren whose connection with the Craft is severed completely are those who are expelled or are invited to resign by the Masonic authorities, pending disciplinary action.

In trying to make sense of my predicament, little did I realise that I was about to embark on a journey of research and enlightenment culminating in this work. Neither did it occur to me that I might uncover some facts that had not only been carefully obscured from the general public but primarily from the Masons themselves. It was probably because I was not looking for secrets that I found them, since many false trails had been laid for those who were specifically searching for them. One will not find secrets inside a box where the label outside proclaims "secrets inside"!

As well as delving into areas such as history, sociology and psychology, this research has taken me into some very interesting subject areas such as stage hypnosis and the extent to which the Internet is utilised. On the Internet, the most modern of inventions, I was surprised to find the ancient fraternity of Freemasons represented as early as 1998 when there were only handful of Masonic websites and the Internet Lodge started with members communicating through email with actual meetings held a few times a year in different locations. In 2004 when I next checked there were over 10,000 websites and today (2011), a search on the term 'Freemasonry' indicates that there now over two million web references. There is even a Masonic Lodge in the 3-D virtual world of 'Second Life' where people are represented by cartoon-like avatars operated from computers that could be anywhere in the world.

Alt.freemasonry is a "newsgroup", which is a publicly accessible discussion forum, where anybody can post written messages and get replies from one or more people, but where the vast majority of subscribers stay anonymous and simply "listen in" to the "conversations". The type of discussions going on at any time would include enthusiastic masons arguing with hostile anti-masons, people thinking of joining asking questions, new members that feel they want to announce themselves to the world and other non-secret issues such as Masonic history or the latest book on the subject. Even this book in its electronic form has been discussed where some contributors refuse to read it but still feel qualified to criticise it.

Although this book can be read as a commentary on modern Freemasonry, it is really a record of the path I took through the mass of data that eventually enabled me to break the Masonic spell. For this reason, it does not explore any particular subject area such as the Origins of Freemasonry or the "Is Freemasonry a religion?" debate in as much depth as one can find in other books. Similarly, I have not been interested in exposing corruption in high places (even though some prospective publishers asked me to do so) nor do I examine in any depth how groups of Masons can collude to the disadvantage others.

As part of this research, I have covered subjects which at first seem far removed from Freemasonry in order to draw out the parallels against which Freemasonry can be been measured. What is unique compared to previous authors in this arena, is the blend of this information with my own inside observations and experiences. Put simply, it is a matter of looking at the wood AND the trees. As an example, where Stephen Knight reprinted the text of the initiation ceremony as an appendix to his book, "The Brotherhood", 1984, which by itself is not very interesting to non-masons, I have shared with the reader the experience and feelings of the candidate as he undergoes this rather frightening ordeal.

Martin Short, "Inside the Brotherhood", 1989, reported that top Masons were "scared stiff" that Stephen Knight had tumbled their secrets and that it was only a matter of time before he reached the heart of the matter. That they breathed a sigh of relief when he died, means that he did not quite get there. Short's work takes us a bit closer and although he marshalled many relevant facts together, there were still missing pieces of this jigsaw that only someone who has gone through the Masters chair could supply.

"We have nothing to hide and certainly nothing to be ashamed of, but we object to having our affairs investigated by outsiders" (Grand Lodge Quarterly Communication, June 1981), so presumably it is okay for insiders to conduct an inquiry? Guy Arnold, "Brain Wash", 1992, illustrates the

difficulty with this position since while those outside any closed system do not have enough information to challenge, those inside who could mount a challenge, are often unable, for instance in the case of government secrecy, by being bound by the Official Secrets Act.

John Stalker who was given an assignment to investigate whether there was a "shoot to kill" policy in Northern Ireland believes that as he got closer to the truth and his enquiries became uncomfortable for those in authority, he was discredited and removed from the job before he got too close ("Stalker", 1988). Arnold comments that those who present a danger to a system by stepping outside the accepted limits of conformity have to be discredited and their influence destroyed. This is often done by appeals to loyalty, by ignoring, by sneering and by casting doubts on their arguments with faint praise. Grand Lodge will attempt to achieve this by instructing the rank and file Brethren, through the formal organ of the Quarterly Communications, which is distributed to all Masons, and additionally, by the high ranking Masons that visit most Lodge meetings to deliver messages on behalf Grand Lodge, not to allow themselves to become exposed to these types of works.

Freemasons in Publishing or in the Media are unlikely to become involved with its distribution, not so much because they might disagree with the content, but mainly because of a passage in a booklet called "Information for the guidance of members of the Craft", 1987. This threatens them with "disciplinary methods" for committing the Masonic offence of preparing, publishing, selling or circulating works which purport to give particulars of the secrets and inner proceedings.

I met with this barrier in 1994 when I first floated the idea of this book and so I went on to publish the first edition in electronic format. Another example of this happened to author Dominic Torr, a retired member of the British Diplomatic Service, who has used his extensive knowledge of espionage to write a number of popular spy novels even selling movie rights of one to Peter Ustinov. Torr researched Freemasonry after - he explains in a foreword to his fourth spy novel "Hoodwink" - coming across the wrongful dismissal of a non-Mason partner from one of London's leading legal firms where all the other partners were Masons. So he decided to give a Masonic background to "Hoodwink". The story involves villains taking advantage of the cloak of Masonic secrecy that allowed them to carry out their evil deeds away from prying eyes. In the end, the principles of Freemasonry were upheld and the villains got their just desserts.

Unable to find a major publisher for the book despite his previous publications, Torr was having "Hoodwink" published by a small firm in 1997. A trial one hundred copies had been printed when the publisher told him publication had to be abandoned because the printer was being bankrupted. But not before one copy had come into the possession of Grand Lodge. The Quatuor Coronati Lodge in London, a lodge devoted to Masonic research, published a review of "Hoodwink" by a D.M. Kalman in their 1997 annual volume of research essays but requests for a copy of this review still remain unanswered.

In 2009 Torr was urged to try again to get the book published but this time too, he says he could find neither an agent nor a major publisher. Although "Hoodwink" has now (February 2011) been published by another small firm and is getting an encouraging reception by readers and small book sellers, it has not had (at the time of writing) a single review from the media, and Torr has been attacked on the Internet - in what appears to be an attempt to bury the book one Mr. E King (webmaster of Grand Lodge of Maine's website and self-nominated crusader against anti-masons) who has been posting negative reviews of Torr's book on his website (masonicinfo.com) and on sites like amazon.com trying to persuade people not to read the book – even though ultimately Freemasonry is shown in the book as being a force for good.

I must point out that 'Freemasonry Inside Out' is not an attack on individual Masons (far from it in fact) nor is it opposed to the basic beliefs of Freemasonry although I now have the 'honour' of also being listed on King's website as an anti-mason. It must be said though that not all Masons are happy with King's rantings and one has openly written to him saying *"You take people who oppose the institution, and then attack them as individuals. Rather than explaining why their arguments are invalid, you instead claim they have mental problems, personal issues, and seek to embarrass them personally on a global scale. It is dishonorable. It is unethical. It is beneath us, and runs contrary to what we stand for"* (freemasonrywatch.com).

I personally have always believed that the practice of charity as well as the social interaction were positive aspects of Freemasonry. What I have questioned is why this is mixed up with secret rituals and make-believe history. Therefore this work is more aimed at exposing the "hidden agenda" of Freemasonry as an institution rather than any individual masons or their beliefs. For many it will leave a bad taste. As Commander Michael Higham, previous Grand Secretary, has said, *"We have been offered the fruits of objective journalism before, only to find they were bitter fruit indeed'*.

Many members will undoubtedly experience emotions ranging from embarrassment and disillusionment to anger and betrayal. Some of these men (Masonic "fundamentalists") would, if they could, take their "revenge" in spiteful, anonymous ways using their influential commercial positions to settle scores. One of Knight's Masonic informers provided a graphic account how a man can be ruined who has fallen foul of the Brethren. Such is the power of the ritual, most Masons and ex-Masons are paranoid enough to believe that the traditional barbaric penalties would be visited upon them if they should ever break their Oath of secrecy.

In 1826, a New York bricklayer who was preparing a book revealing the organisation's secrets mysteriously disappeared. Rumours of his murder at the hands of the Masons swept through America and caused such uproar that it became the basis of a new political party actually called the Anti-Masonic Party.

I hope that Bro A G Markham, who wrote the inaugural paper for the Transactions of Quatuor Coronati Lodge, 1997, doesn't lump me together with the journalists who in his opinion only write anti-Masonic stories when they have nothing else to write about. It has taken me many years to work the psychological stranglehold of the Masonic Oath out of my system. Producing this work has enabled me to lay this particular ghost to rest. Ian Haworth, anti-cult campaigner, points out that for most people it is impossible, and takes far more than just courage, to be the one person to stand up and challenge the system. Arnold suggests that only an "odd man out" can upset the pattern and disrupt the easy process of manipulation of the majority.

The strength and will to produce this work is based on a belief that men should not be taken advantage of in the name of the Supreme Being, as well as an honest application of the fundamental Masonic principles of Brotherly Love, Charity and above all else, Truth.

Hugh McFarland, 2011

Readers' Comments

Thank you to those readers who have provided feedback and extra internet links. These are very much appreciated. There are over 400 internet links embedded in the text of this book which were all functioning at the time of publication. Inevitably over time some of these will change in which case Google should help you find an alternative source. Below is a sample of the many reviews readers have sent me. Please feel free to write to me direct at mcfarland.hugh@gmail.com with any comments you wish to add.

"If you want to know all about Freemasonry this is the book to read. Written by a former member of the Masons the information is written from experience and is quite an eye-opener." **Mrs. GP, North Wales UK**

"Excellent work on many levels! Excellent research, excellent reasoning, even though much data is presented the argument is very focused, and the point and ultimate subject is of no secondary importance to anyone - a wakeup call to re-examine the doctrines that many have been taking for granted. I was presented with an opportunity to join and am very glad I had a chance to read your book first. I am very thankful to you for helping people like myself to save a lot of time and resources in arriving at an informed decision about masonry. Many thanks!" **AP, California**

"A very interesting and informative read! I have always been intrigued by freemasonry, the secret codewords, handshakes etc. Members of my immediate family are

Masons. I have been encouraged to ask to join but always needed to know what I was letting myself in for. This book has given me the opportunity to now make an informed decision. Thanks." **GH**

"This rare work breaks the curious all but total silence about Freemasonry following the failure of the House of Commons Home Affairs Committee's 1999 report on Freemasonry in the police and judiciary to achieve compulsory registration of membership in such occupations. Today both media and politicians are reluctant to be the first to come out with criticism - however well-founded - of this prestigious, wealthy, and powerful institution whose titular head is a Royal Duke. This despite - as Grand Lodge admits - some abuse is inevitable given that it has an estimated 350,000 members in all walks of life whose names are a closely kept secret.

Indeed this study of the Craft is long overdue - the last that I know of is Martin Short's "Inside the Brotherhood" (hardback 1989, paperback 1995). That followed Stephen Knight's best selling "The Brotherhood" (1984). What makes Hugh McFarland's book even more rare is that it is written by the past Worshipful Master of a lodge. I can find no other book by a Mason of long standing which gives frank, objective, inside information about the Craft and what it is like to be a Freemason. This is because of the psychological power of the famous oath and fear of the consequences of breaking it - something which McFarland explores. As a student of Freemasonry myself, I cannot too strongly recommend Freemasonry Inside Out for Freemasons and everyone interested in Freemasonry not only in the UK but worldwide." **Filolie, UK**

"I was impressed by the way 'Freemasonry Inside-Out' explained things in a short and concise way and is not simply a summary of other anti-masonic books but the result of a *personal process of weeding out some true facts from the mass of lies and spurious theories. Thank you for providing a short, deep, qualified, interesting and trustworthy overview of the subject. When someone asks me about which book to read to get the information they need to make up their own mind, I will recommend your book as it fits that purpose perfectly."* **JT, Germany**

"'Freemasonry Inside-Out' is an authoritative, well argued, comprehensively sourced and an extremely well written account of the 'possible' dark side of Freemasonry. However, the sobering quality of the cogent arguments makes for healthy self questioning, introspection and a vital examination of one's own motives and intentions. What 'Freemasonry Inside-Out' did do is keep me up all night reading it voraciously. Well written and argued it is. What is has also done is make me rethink, and a period of reflection will direct my thoughts to closer examination of the ritual and what I am doing it all for. The whistle stop tour of the known history is succinct, and well worth reading by all Brethren" **ST, London**

"Lots to absorb here. Well done on a lot of research. As a software/mechanical engineer, I'm used to lots of information on my projects. As a 'young brother' - 4 years - I'm disappointed at the lack of knowledge my 'elders' seem to have about the craft beyond the ritual and the festive board." **KP**

"I will soon be the Master of my Lodge having been in for over 20 years. A lot of the points you make ring true. Having read the majority of the more conventional Masonic books, I had still wondered about the two main points you raise, namely why is there such a strong allegiance to something that seems to have no purpose and where does all the money go." **LW**

"I have found initial reading to be very interesting. As a committed Christian married to a Freemason, I have very mixed feelings about Freemasonry. So I suppose you could say I have a lot of vested interest in knowing more, but as a woman, I am excluded from knowing too much. I think the thing that bothers me more than anything is that it encourages my husband to keep secrets from me, in a relationship that is otherwise based very much on openness and honesty. I suspected, much as you have confirmed, that Freemasonry is full of good and kind people at lower levels who genuinely think that they belong to a fraternity aimed at the common good. I also suspected that, at higher levels, it had certain sinister elements. Many thanks - and thank you for having the courage to write this book." **Mrs AF**

"I have read this very thought provoking book and you may just have changed my mind. I was "invited" to join and I am just going through the lead up to initiation. I now notice some of the recruitment tactics as you described. I am thinking long and hard about it all. Thanks." **MB**

"'Freemasonry Inside-Out' has provided me with abundant information and given me the confidence to make an informed decision whether or not to join. Thank you for writing such a well researched and written book." **IF, Scotland**

"A very interesting and informative book. I had lots of questions regarding rituals, secrets etc. since I become a MM. As you have mentioned in your book, when I asked questions in the Lodge to other brethren, always the same answer "you will learn in due course". You have touched the subject of religious belief and masonry, but I am still in dilemma as my church does not recognize freemasonry." **EH**

"I found 'Freemasonry Inside-Out' to be extremely informative.

It appears that Freemasonry in general has been structured primarily to preserve its own survival through constant funding by its members. This in itself is not necessarily a bad thing as every organization needs to pay the rent and the light bill, etc. Being a social club and charitable organization provides justification enough for its existence as far as it goes, but are there no spiritual practices for the advancement of the inner self involved at all? Without that it would seem rather empty philosophically, somehow." **DMF, San Francisco**

"Even after reading your book I had my initiation last night, but with an insight into what was going to happen it was not the scary event it could have been. I thank you for your info and as I progress through the Craft I will refer back to your book several *times just to keep my feet on the ground."***AS**

"I found this book very very interesting and will reread a number of times I'm sure. I think the 'characteristics' of the cult describe, to varying degrees, the fundamental dynamics of many organised groups in society. Certainly any liberal thinking follower of organised religion will identify with those same 'characteristics' that are employed by the church. While Freemasonry declares that Truth is a personal experience/belief rather than demanding adherence to unquestionable dogma, most organised religions declare they are the guardians of Absolute Truth - which though appearing to be benign and altruistic represents the ultimate suppression and subordination. Naturally, anything (such as Freemasonry) that challenges fundamentalism and embraces tolerance and diversity naturally becomes the enemy." **RMcL, New Zealand**

"I joined the craft in May last year, I could have joined 11 years previous, but felt I knew too little and was too immature at that time. Since then, I have had questions that I have

sought answers to pertaining to Freemasonry, and after reading books readily available by present Freemasons, those questions have by and large remained unanswered. From what I have read of 'Freemasonry Inside-Out', I have learned that I have to keep asking the questions if I am to make any headway in my further studies of freemasonry. The craft is not something, which like some members of my lodge, I just 'do', I want to be a good and faithful Mason, and I believe that from what I have read so far, that this book will help weed out deception from fact.'' **KJ**

1) My Story

When members of my family repeatedly suggested, that if I asked them to invite me into Freemasonry, they would be happy to recommend me, I finally agreed to give it a go. The people I knew that were in it all seemed to be fairly reasonable chaps. I did not think for one minute that any of them would be involved in anything sinister. They talked about the social benefits and the charitable work and intimated that there could be business benefits as well. On top of this, I was intrigued to find out what all this secrecy was about and thought that by joining, all would be revealed. However, as every Mason knows, this is not the case. You have to progress up through each level in order to be told a bit more of the so-called "secrets".

I steadily persevered through the various levels eventually becoming the Worshipful Master of my Lodge. That took some 20 years. I describe below certain dramatic events that led me to give up this time-consuming hobby in the middle of my year as Master and the reason this book came about.

After I left, when non-masons occasionally asked me about the ritual I found I still felt strongly obligated by my Masonic Oaths not to reveal anything at all, even though I considered it to be harmless mumbo-jumbo, which could be found in almost any public library.

This uncomfortable restraining influence bothered me a bit and I spent some time thinking about it. As I browsed through my old Masonic books and papers, I discovered to my amazement, a flaw in the initiation ceremony that convinced me that I was never legitimately bound by the terms of the Masonic Oath in the first place.

Freed from this psychological shackle, I revisited much of what I had previously blindly accepted but with new vision and new questions. I analysed the ritual, the institution's history, the hierarchy and the role of charity. I also studied allied subjects such as early English history, psychology, sociology, hypnosis and cult behaviour, amongst other things.

I am aware that my main conclusions could be shattering for Freemasonry particularly as it appears to be struggling to maintain recruitment levels. I believe that there is a secret buried in Freemasonry but so far those searching for it have been looking in the wrong place and it is not the general public that have been kept in the dark but the "rank and file" members themselves.

So what was it that happened to cause me to walk out of my Lodge while I was still Master - something almost unheard of in Freemasonry? And what happened to me afterwards that persuaded me to write this book?

After a Mason has been through his three degree ceremonies and been a regular member of the Lodge for a few years, he is given his first official job which is that of Steward (basically to serve wine to the other brethren at the meal following the ceremony). That is the first rung of the ladder leading to the Masters Chair. It was the custom in my Lodge that when a Mason is appointed to this role he is also invited to attend the General Purposes Committee (GPC) for that year – the next time he becomes a formal member of this committee is many years later when he becomes the Junior Warden, two levels below Master. The GPC is made up of the Master, the Senior and Junior Wardens, Past Masters and those holding non-ritual offices such as Secretary, Treasurer and Charity Steward. It makes decisions about the programme for the year, hears applications for membership, plans the Ladies Night, discusses how it will deal with brethren who cannot afford fees, etc.

As a newly appointed Steward, my attendance at the GPC was the first time I was able to observe many of these senior brethren close up, conducting business outside of the formal Lodge meetings. You can imagine my astonishment when an argument broke out between the Secretary and the Treasurer, who normally sit beside each other in the Lodge and always appeared to be in perfect harmony with each other, that got so heated that the Treasurer actually got out of his seat and physically attacked the Secretary, grabbing him by the throat until other members intervened and calmed the situation down. So much for Brotherly Love! It was obvious to me that there was a history between these two that caused small problems to flare up and become major issues. Little did I know back then how this feud would affect me personally and play a major role in my leaving the Lodge many years later.

About ten years later, when I was next a member of the GP committee, the same Secretary and Treasurer were still in post. When I was nominated as Master Elect, the committee needed to know from me who I was planning to appoint to the various non-ritual offices, such as Secretary, Treasurer, Chaplain, Charity Steward, etc. The custom was that unless one of these officers offered to stand down, or the incoming Master had very strong reasons to appoint others, then existing officers were usually reappointed which was why the Secretary and Treasurer were still there. As for the ritual based officers, these generally automatically moved up one level with the outgoing Master becoming a Past Master and creating a gap at the bottom for a new Steward. It is the Secretary of the Lodge who works with the Master Elect to advise him on protocol and guide him to make the correct decisions about the running of the Lodge – for example the appointment of a member of the Lodge to his first formal role as a Steward and so commence his journey to eventually become Master of the Lodge.

The person who was next in line to be appointed wrote to me to say that although he anticipated that I would invite him to become a Steward, he would prefer it if I did not actually appoint him. This was because becoming a Steward required weekly attendance at the Lodge of Instruction (LOI) where members meet, usually in a room above a pub, and learn and practice the ritual and it is an obligation for the Stewards to attend. His reason simply was that he was in a junior league football team and his football practice sessions clashed with the LOI meeting days. He said that he would be very grateful if I passed over him this year and he promised to take up the role in the next year with the Master who was due to follow me. He also requested that I didn't mention his request to his father who might not be too happy about it and who would likely try to persuade him against his decision – his father happened to be the Treasurer.

I sought the Secretary's advice about this matter and we decided to go with the young Mason's request. Later when I had to announce the list of my new officers to the GPC, the Treasurer was most unhappy to learn that his son was not on the list. I explained that his son had made the request not to be included and also that he didn't wish me to discuss it with his father. The Treasurer became extremely angry that I had not broken his son's confidence and come to talk to him about this and announced his belief that I had been naively put up to this by the Secretary as a way of getting back at him. Then he stormed out of the meeting.

Apparently the Treasurer had shrewdly planned his son's initiation into the Lodge years ago so that in the twenty years it took to become Master, it would coincide with the Lodge's centenary year which would be a very prestigious event to preside over. The Master would receive many invitations to visit other Lodges up and down the country to talk about his own Lodge's history and naturally he would take his father with him as his guest. There would also a large charity social to celebrate the centenary to which many Masonic dignitaries would be invited to. The Treasurer had dreamed of this day and now it had been snatched away from him because I had let his son slip back a year and this was the real reason he was so angry. I gave it no more thought, what was done was done and maybe the next master might be able to shuffle things around to satisfy the Treasurer's desire that he and his son should play an integral role during the Lodge's centenary year.

The Treasurer, was quite a senior figure within the Province having had Masonic honours awarded to him (which some members attributed to his generous donations to the Masonic charities) and because of his senior rank, he was often invited to attend other Lodges as their guest. It is also the custom within the Province that Masters of other Lodges would invite the new Master to visit their Lodges also as a guest. I noticed that I wasn't getting many invitations and word got back to me that during the Treasurer's many visits to other Lodges he was telling other Masters not to invite me and was being a bit unkind about my attributes as a Master.

I really wasn't too bothered about this but I mentioned it to the Secretary. It surprised and angered me to learn that not only was the Secretary fully aware of this but he had taken it upon himself, without asking me, to report this matter on my behalf to the Masonic authorities. It was obvious to me that this feud between the Secretary and the Treasurer was getting out of hand and that I was being used as a ping pong ball between them.

About the same time, I had what started out as a minor accident and tore a ligament in my ankle which resulted in having my leg in plaster for six weeks. I did not let this get in the way of everyday activities and it must have been quite comical to see me in the Lodge with my plaster cast leg sticking out in front of the pedestal.

The day before the plaster was due to come off, something awful happened. It was about midnight and I was in the bathroom before retiring to bed when I was overcome with a very odd sensation. The best way to describe it was like I had just sat down on a seat in the bus having had to run hard to catch it but not being very fit so that my heart was pounding away and my breathing was very laboured. But the only strenuous thing I had been doing was brushing my teeth. I struggled to the bedroom and my wife called the emergency doctor who asked me to describe my symptoms to him. He suggested that I might have been having a panic attack to which I replied "too right am I panicking" and that he better get round to me very fast.

By the time the doctor arrived, I felt that my body had calmed down quite a bit and maybe this was some passing incident. He took my pulse and told me that my heart rate was still over 200 beats per minute which was very dangerous unless you are a fit athlete – normal heart rate for a man is about 70. God knows what my rate had shot up to when this thing first hit me. The doctor made a quick phone call and then asked quite casually if I would be happy to go to the hospital for a check-up and if I was ok about it, we could go now even though it was after midnight. What I did not realise at the time was that he was actually organising for a crash team to be on standby with all sorts of specialists that were on-call to be available plus he called for an ambulance with flashing lights to whisk me off to the hospital.

It turned out that I had a deep vein thrombosis (DVT), a blood clot in my leg that had broken away and travelled through my heart to my lungs where it had knocked out one lung. This was called a pulmonary embolism (PE). Because of the 50% reduction in oxygen supply, my body had reacted automatically by making my heart rate shoot up and with rapid short breaths in an attempt to compensate for the reduced lung function.

Apparently it is this reaction of the heart that can often be fatal. Looking back, I think I was saved by adopting a breathing pattern which I used in the gym while pushing weights that enabled maximum oxygen intake. A DVT and resulting PE can occur after long periods of inactivity and is usually known as 'economy class syndrome' because of the many air passengers that get struck down with this. After many tests and getting blood thinning drugs pumped into me and breathing with the aid of an oxygen mask, I was taken to a hospital ward where I stayed for about two weeks. I only really became aware of the seriousness of my situation on the second day when the plaster cast technician came to my bed to remove the plaster. He explained to me that this was a very rare event that can happen to people in plaster and thankfully over the course of his fifteen year career he had only lost two of his patients this way. I told him how glad I was for him that I had not ruined his track record!

As one can imagine, events such as this can change one's outlook on life quite significantly and in my case I wanted to make sure that I did not waste valuable time on trivial things because we really do not know have much time we have left on earth and there are so many more constructive things to do. I felt that Freemasonry was taking up far too much time and that I should be spending more quality time with my family and friends.

I also found that I tended to act more spontaneously and not let opportunities pass by to do unusual things that caught my interest. One such example was that I noticed a small ad in 'The Stage', a newspaper for the performing arts industry, for an introductory course on Stage Hypnosis. I had always been fascinated by these hypnotists who seemed to be able to get ordinary people to do some amazing things at the click of their fingers so I registered for this course at quite a considerable cost.

It turned out that this course was run by the same person who had first trained the world renowned celebrity hypnotist, Paul McKenna. This two day course was a real eye-opener - it shocked me to discover the similarities between hypnotic induction techniques and the Masonic ritual. With this insight and together with my own knowledge of behavioural conditioning (my academic degree is in Experimental Psychology), I was getting very uncomfortable with the idea of administering what might be hypnotic inductions to unsuspecting candidates that were convinced they were doing certain things of their own free will as well giving their total trust to me and the other participants in the ritual to take care of them.

I decided to test the Secretary on the strength of his Masonic beliefs to help me decide whether I should confide in him or not. It is a fundamental principle, if not 'The' fundamental principal, that every Freemason should believe in a divine being. I called the Secretary over and told him that I had a problem – I told him that I didn't believe in God anymore and asked him what I should do about this. The correct answer would have been that I should leave the Lodge. He seemed rather surprised that anybody could actually come to the conclusion that there was no God but never-the-less his advice was that I should keep quiet about it and not to mention this to anyone else as it could cause serious problems for the Lodge. This told me all I needed to know about his attitude to a main tenet of Freemasonry.

Having decided that I didn't want to play this "crafty trick" on the new recruits and draw them into a lifelong commitment to the Brotherhood, I knew that I needed to get out of it. On the other hand, I didn't want to enter into any debate with any of the Masons in my Lodge or indeed the Masonic authorities who would soon be demanding an explanation from me as to why I was doing the unheard of and disruptive thing of resigning while

I was still Master of the Lodge. In my opinion, it would have been a fruitless task anyway since in my view all of these people would have been conditioned to not listen objectively to what I had to say.

I realised that the conflict between the Secretary and Treasurer involving me, gave me a great opportunity to mix things up a bit and engineer a way out of this situation. I wrote to both of them to say that this conflict between them that had dragged me into it, needed to be resolved. That required both of them apologising to me and to each other. I pointed out that the ritual stated that if there was an argument in the Lodge then one or both of the parties had to withdraw from the Lodge and settle their differences so that harmony could once again be restored. I told them that if they did not sort out this problem then they would leave me no option but to be the one withdrawing from the Lodge and that I would write to the GPC and tender my resignation.

Needless to say, neither man had the balls to step forward, still blaming the other for the problems and thinking my threat was a hollow bluff. It was therefore against this background that I tendered my resignation explaining that a situation had arisen in the Lodge that caused disharmony and despite my attempts to fix the problem, it appeared to be insurmountable and therefore it left me no option but to be the one to withdraw in order to restore harmony.

I knew when the Secretary read my letter to the GPC, which he was obliged to do, that all hell would break out but neither he nor the Treasurer would be man enough to explain to the committee their role in the saga.

I went away for the weekend as I knew there would be a flurry of phone calls – some people thought I was really resigning because I couldn't cope with the amount of ritual I would have to administer and kindly offered to take on some of the burden, others thought I had been affected psychologically by my health problem and suggested counselling and one or two told me I was committing Masonic suicide. The overall clamour was for me to come and finish my year as Master and then leave quietly because walking out in the middle of the year gave the Lodge quite an administrative problem and the previous Master was not happy at all about the prospect of having to come back and take over the ritual from me for the rest of the year.

As expected, I got a call from the Provincial Grand Lodge to come and visit and have a friendly chat about the 'problem'. When I got there it turned out to be more of an inquisition than a chat. There were four men sitting across a boardroom table from me – the Assistant Provincial Grand Master and three other high ranking Masons, one of which I remember was the Chief Executive of a major high street bank and the others were of similar standing in the outside world. It was quite an intimidating experience.

Firstly they tried to use their authority in quite an aggressive way to command me to go back to my position and at least finish the year. I just kept explaining that as much as I would like to, the ritual itself required me to resign because of the disharmony and I felt it was my Masonic duty to rigidly follow the ritual. Unlike the Secretary, when I confronted him about my belief or not in a divine being, these men couldn't be seen to say to me in a minuted formal meeting that the ritual wasn't really that important enough to follow so religiously.

They then tried a different approach. One of these men produced a letter which he put down on the table facing him. Being able to read upside down, I could see that they had prepared a letter of resignation for the Treasurer! They asked me that if the Treasurer were to resign, would that enable me to go back into the Lodge and finish the year. It was plainly obvious to me that they had this fall back plan already discussed with the Treasurer where they had probably promised him a position in another Lodge with some Masonic promotion to sweeten the pill. I told them that it would not be very Masonic of me to force the resignation of another Brother – they had had their chance to solve the problem and now I had no choice.

I knew that while I stayed on this wicket, they didn't have any chance of bowling me out but if I was to introduce the real reason for my actions then I would be in uncharted territory and that they might find a way to knock me off course and I did not want to take that chance. After quite a few hours of getting nowhere, they reluctantly agreed that I could go without any further pressure from them to change my mind.

Before the meeting finished, they commented that although they thought I was taking the ritual a bit too literally and they were disappointed that they couldn't persuade me on a different course of action, they were glad to observe that I didn't harbour any negative thoughts towards the craft and they invited me to stay for lunch. I'm sure they considered that I was a bit deranged and beyond help.

Now that we had got the nasty business of my resignation out of the way, the lunch was very cordial and everyone seemed friendly enough. I was sat next to the Assistant Provincial Grand Master. A person in his position is inundated with invitations to visit other Lodges – some for lunch time meetings and others in the evenings. I asked him how he chose what Lodges to visit as he surely couldn't please everybody. He told me it was very simple – he studied the menus, if he was having fish for lunch then he wanted to go somewhere that was serving meat in the evening and vice versa. The Lodges that he visits regard it as a great honour if he accepts their invitation and he is treated like royalty when he goes there – little do they know it's all down to his stomach.

We chatted a lot about non-Masonic things such as my work, sports, holidays, etc. Something happened a short time later and it took a while for the significance of this to become apparent. The company I worked for at that time, based in the North West of England, was invited, out-of-the blue, to tender for a computerised membership system to be installed in Freemasons Hall, the 'head office' of English Freemasonry. Nothing was said but I wondered at the time whether our company was selected because of my Masonic links and maybe they didn't know yet that I had already resigned and was not their favourite person.

This contract would have been very lucrative for the company and a lot of work was done to try to win the tender. The company was very confident about winning because they were market leaders in this particular field, their solution was a 100% fit to the specification and it was the most price competitive. As the company was getting 'positive noises' about their almost certain acceptance, the company invested significantly in resources and bespoke customising. Then just as the company thought they had got everything sown up they were informed, again out-of-the-blue, that they had been dropped from the tender process without any further explanation or communication. Was it that my issues with my Lodge had now surfaced at Grand Lodge and they decided to distance themselves from me or was it part of a more cynical plan, hatched when the Assistant Provincial Grand Master fished for certain information about my work during that lunch, so that I could be punished some time later by dangling a lucrative opportunity only then to snatch it away as demonstration of what the future could have been if I had not rocked the boat or more seriously, an attempt to ruin the company? Of course when this kind of thing happens one never has any proof.

When I left Freemasonry, I had no intention of writing a book but as I explain elsewhere, despite leaving Freemasonry and having somewhat negative attitudes about the ritual, I found I was still to some extent conditioned by the Oath even though on an academic level I knew exactly what was going on. It was in trying to understand and resolve this conundrum that I started researching and this book evolved suggesting that perhaps we have all been hoodwinked into the longest running pyramid scam the world has known.

2) Overview

Those who have pursued the "secrets" of Freemasonry have been led down blind alleys following signposts to non-existent landmarks, whilst others, who focus on attempting to demonstrate that corruption in business and high office is linked with Freemasonry, unknowingly divert their readers' attention away from the real issues. These typical strands of enquiry have ironically, helped Freemasonry to keep certain information secret for over two and a half centuries.

The veil of secrecy that surrounds the order not only prevents independent external analysis but is also designed to keep its own members from discovering certain information about the organisation in general and the Masonic ritual in particular.

Most Masons are nice ordinary chaps who got drawn into freemasonry through their friends, family or business contacts usually with the unspoken promise of social and business advancement.

New members are just as curious as the general public in wanting to know what Freemasonry is really about. Their eager questions are met with responses that indicate that all will be revealed in time. They assume that as they move up the Masonic ladder their questions will be answered. What actually happens is that they gradually stop asking questions.

Those who have doubts about the fraternity are trapped by the dilemma of being prevented from discussing these topics with outsiders due to the powerful psychological effect of the Masonic Oath. But at the same time, they find themselves unable to raise these issues with senior Freemasons because they would not only view their doubts as disloyal and almost blasphemous but would remind them that they entered Masonry of their own free will and that "once a Mason, always a Mason".

To the outside world, Freemasonry projects an image that it is an organisation dedicated to the teaching of high moral principles which it demonstrates by making large donations to non-Masonic charities. Most Masons believe this as well, and will strongly defend Freemasonry on this basis if challenged.

Previous estimates of the number of Freemasons in the UK put this figure at 750,000 - about 1 in 20 of the adult male population. Recent figures from the Grand Lodge of England put this figure at 350,000 members in over 8600 lodges. This means an average number of 90 members per lodge, however, many men are members of more than one lodge and this could explain the differences in the various estimates. The report also shows that there were 12,000 new recruits in 1995 which was similar to the 1994 figure. Grand Lodge will not publish a membership list on the basis that Freemasonry is a voluntary organisation that respects the privacy of the members. It also cites the Data Protection Act as requiring the consent of each member before publication can take place.

World-wide, it is estimated that there are almost 5 million members, 3 million of which are in the USA. Robert Lomas (Turning the Hiram Key, 2005) states that *"Freemasonry is the second-largest and best equipped spiritual organisation in the world. It is second only to the Roman Catholic Church as a worldwide spiritual movement"*. This is obviously a very significant group and the air of mystery and secrecy surrounding it, has attracted quite a lot of attention, particularly in recent times when the media has regarded everybody and every group as fair game, especially the Establishment, and in particular the Royal Family.

Freemasonry has been subjected to examination from the point of view of illicit dealings between members carried out under the cloak of privacy that Freemasonry affords. Other views have considered the subject of unfair advantage in career progression in business, the police force and the civil service. Stephen Knight (now deceased), even suggested that Freemasonry was infiltrated by the KGB in order to speed up their members progress through the civil service to the higher echelons of government.

There was a lot of publicity in the 1980's concerning an Italian Masonic Lodge known as P2 which was used as a cover for political subversion which involved the "Vatican Bank" and culminated in Roberto Calvi's untimely death under Blackfriars Bridge in London in June 1982. There are still aspects of this episode rambling on today such as the case of Kroll, the world's largest corporate detective agency, who (after a series of reports including a detailed forensic study that concluded that Calvi had in fact been murdered and not a suicide victim as originally alleged) are suing the Calvi family for $3 million for non-payment of fees (The Observer, 7/8/94).

Exposures which are aimed at illustrating the corrupt nature of some Freemasons, who happen to also hold senior positions in business or in the public sector, tend not to be of very much interest or concern to the average "rank and file" member for the following reasons:

- The men exposed are usually very senior masonically and are held in high esteem, whilst the author of the work is invariably not a Mason and is regarded as yet another "mason basher". The general attitude to the work would be one of "he would say that wouldn't he" and therefore there is very little interest in reading what he has to say.

- If the men exposed are obviously guilty of the charges laid against them, then the attitude taken is one of "in such a large and diverse group involving millions of members spread across the globe, you are bound to have a few bad apples as you would also find in, say, the golf club or the Church".

- The ordinary Masons are unlikely to ever be in a position where they themselves could be involved in corruption or wrongdoing of the scale usually exposed and therefore it is difficult for them to fully appreciate the opportunities that do exist for people who are in that position.

- Business deals amongst brethren is deemed quite acceptable and stories that involve a Masonic advantage are often told light-heartedly across the meal table following Masonic meetings. Likewise, stories of Masons being let off minor offences such as traffic violations by Masonic police officers are similarly regarded.

- Masons regard attacks on senior Freemasons as attacks on the Craft itself and as a member, usually feel obliged to defend it to outsiders particularly as it reflects on their own credibility.

Freemasonry has also attracted a fair amount of study into its origins with suggestions ranging from the operative medieval stone masons, King Solomon's Temple, ancient Egyptians, Rosicrucians, Knights Templars, Essenes, and many others. It is true that there are similarities between the ritual and regalia of these various groups and Freemasonry, but did the ritual evolve or was it copied?

Freemasonry regards itself as a society within a society.

Members often refer to external events as happening in the "outside world" or to the "profane". Its declared aims are that of Brotherly love, charity and truth. Its members are instructed to practice every moral and social virtue. The shroud of secrecy leads many to believe otherwise. More importantly the hallmark of a secret society is one that involves members taking an omerta type oath which, if broken renders a member liable to dire punishment. It is this that makes nonsense of Grand Lodge insistence that "Freemasonry is not a secret society but a private society". Despite this statement, it is obvious that much secrecy does surround the Order and it is usually this aspect which attracts most attention.

There are enough books in the public library today that describe the Masonic ritual, including "Darkness Visible" by Walton Hannah, 1952, "The Brotherhood", 1984, by Stephen Knight, "Born in Blood - The Lost Secrets of Freemasonry" by John Robinson, 1989 and more recently "The Hiram Key" 1996 by freemasons Christopher Knight and Robert Lomas. This is not a new phenomenon though, for Tolstoy (not a Mason) was able to glean enough information from Russian public libraries in the 1800's to fully describe a Russian Masonic initiation ceremony in his novel, War and Peace, 1868. As a point of interest, his account was so accurate that in 1972, a New Zealand Lodge was able to use his text as a basis for carrying out the ceremony in their Lodge. In 1989, a six part documentary on British TV, "Inside the Brotherhood", based on Martin Short's book of the same name, actually re-enacted parts of the ritual for the camera.

There were many "exposures" of Masonic ritual in the early 18th century and these have become some of the most valuable documents to Masonry as they are the only written records that exist from that time. It seems ironic that "*one of the most important books ever published by Quatuor Coronati Lodge*" (a Lodge devoted to historical Masonic research) is

"The Early French Exposures 1737-1751".

A booklet by Lionel Vibert from the early 1900's titled "The Rare Books of Freemasonry" and reprinted by the "Sure Fire Press" in 1987, details the whereabouts of all the known early exposures that includes some intriguing titles such as "The Secrets of the Freemason revealed by a disgusted Brother", 1759, and "The Use and Abuse of Freemasonry: a work of the greatest utility to the Brethren of the society, to mankind in general and to the Ladies in particular", 1783.

In this "exposure", as well as providing a stimulating insight into Freemasonry for the general reader, by weaving a path through the mass of data, highlighting landmarks along the way, Masons will also have some of their unasked questions answered. In order to change perceptions that Masons might have about their fraternity, the first part of the book examines the validity of the Masonic Oath which is the main obstacle to any objective assessment for a practising Mason or ex-Mason. It will attempt to answer the question posed by Robert Lomas in his 2005 book, "Turning the Hiram Key" where he says *"There is a veiled and deep 'something' in those rituals but what is it?"*

The second part deals with subjects such as Masonic charity, history and the higher degrees whereas the third part looks at other types of organisation and religious groups where there are parallels with Freemasonry. The final part brings together the strands of enquiry that enables an answer to the challenging question posed by John Hamill, Librarian and Curator of the United Grand Lodge of England, in his 1986 book, "The Craft", who asks *"If Freemasonry is not a religion, a political force, or a pressure group and if its members do not receive any material gain from their membership, why has it survived for so long and why do so many seek initiation and continue their membership?"*

3) Secrecy & Secrets

The official line is that the secrets of Freemasonry are concerned with its traditional "modes of recognition". There is no secret about any of its aims and principles but like many other societies, it regards some of its internal affairs as private matters for its members.

This seems fair enough, but one does wonder about the extraordinary amount of emphasis placed on secrecy to the extent that much of the secret Masonic ritual is about the need to keep secrecy and the traditional punishments associated with breaking this secrecy. To understand this Masonic paranoia, one has to distinguish between the so-called secrets of Freemasonry and the cloak of secrecy that surrounds Freemasonry.

According to the ritual, the genuine secrets of Freemasonry were lost in biblical times when the mythical master, Hiram Abiff, Master Builder of King Solomon's Temple, was murdered because he "wouldn't and couldn't" reveal the secrets to some ruffians. Much of the ritual is concerned with searching for these ancient secrets and by following certain signs and landmarks they will be rediscovered. The opening ceremony reminds the Brethren that by following their Master's guidance and by their own endeavours they hope to find "that which is lost". In the meantime the Freemasons have substituted these secrets with "signs, tokens and words" (salutes, handshakes and passwords) and this is what is meant by the phrase "modes of recognition".

A common version of the origins of Freemasonry holds that the modern "speculative" Mason evolved out of the medieval "operative" stone-masons who used to travel the country on major building projects, primarily churches and cathedrals. In order to get employment, and to prove their level of skill and hence their level of payment, the stone-masons used secret "modes of recognition".

An article by A C F Jackson on Masonic Passwords, printed in the "Transactions of Quatuor Coronati Lodge - 1974", points out that passwords were not introduced into Freemasonry until approximately 1730, some thirteen years after the formation of the Grand Lodge and at least a hundred years after the first known lodges, those being the "Acception" Lodge meeting in London in 1621 and a Lodge meeting in Warrington in to which Elias Ashmole (founder of the Ashmoleon Museum in Oxford in 1682) was initiated in 1646.

He explains that Masons used to hold processions in the street and appear in theatrical performances in full Masonic regalia. The names of distinguished initiates were given to the newspapers and there was a general air of openness about everything except the secret ceremonies. The general public, though, were particularly interested in the secret aspects and from about 1723, a number of publications were produced, collectively known as Masonic Exposures, that purported to provide the secrets.

Jackson believes that the passwords were introduced following the publication of various exposures, such as "The Whole Institutions of Free Masons Opened", 1725, and "Masonry Dissected", 1730, as a defence against non-Masons and other "secret enemies" armed with the secrets of the ritual who might try to gain unauthorised entry. However, quickly following the introduction of passwords into the ritual, another exposure "Three Distinct Knocks", 1760, then gave these passwords away.

Trevor Stewart also points out (in his introduction to Hutchinson's 1775 book, "The Spirit of Masonry"), that the ceremonies themselves never used to have secrecy as a fundamental principle but it was probably because of ridicule in the popular press of that time, that secrecy was introduced.

In the 1980s, when Freemasonry was again receiving unwelcome attention because of its secrecy and the suspected ease with which it can be abused, Grand Lodge arranged for the Craft to combat this by opening its doors just a little. This apparent "glasnost" was important in helping to combat the attempt in 1997/1998 by the House of Commons Home affairs Committee enquiring into Freemasonry to force judges, police and some other public servants to declare their membership.

Freemasonry also started publishing pamphlets, books, videos, CDs, and even showing some of its ceremonies on TV. It has created a permanent exhibition; open to the public, that in 1992 attracted 21,951 visitors. In another PR stunt, in May 1993, The Princess of Wales attended a performance of Mozart's Masonic opera, "The Magic Flute" in Freemasons Hall. As Freemasons Hall was not licensed for public performances, elaborate arrangements were made so that tickets could be sold to the general public without breaking the law. Individual Freemasons themselves, however, would be the first to admit that the PR machine is actually giving away precious little of its internal workings.

Another example is that in March 2005, Lewis Masonic, publishers of Masonic books, announced that after 200 years of secrecy, Masonic books are to go on sale through high street bookshops. Their press release claims that their decision to open their book titles to the public "has taken the book world by storm". But the only sort of works on offer included books on Masonic speech making and theories about the origins. Despite the press release claims, it was another whitewash, as in reality nothing secret was put into the public domain.

What follows next is a collection of different views relating to Masonic secrecy culled from various other books and publications that illustrate the wide range of opinions and confusion among Masonic and other commentators:-

- Many cults have secrecy as a prerequisite for anyone studying their system. The argument used is that the novice could not possibly explain it correctly - it had to be experienced to be understood and descriptions simply lead to distortions. Canon Tydeman, quoted by Martin Short, compares attempts to convey the joys of Freemasonry to non-masons to that of trying to describe motherhood to spinsters.

- Freemasons regard their membership as a privilege and their knowledge as privileged information.

- C. W. Leadbeater, "The Hidden Life in Freemasonry", 1926, warns Masons against discussing in public, any aspect of the ceremonies, even the non-secret parts, in case inquisitive and intelligent bystanders deduce more than they ought to know.

- Concerning the bloody punishments a Freemason can expect for breaking his Oath of secrecy, Leadbeater justifies the extreme solemnity by pointing out that in the middle ages, Masons could have been put to death for their beliefs and therefore the whole group were at risk should just one person break their Oath.

- From "Masonic Law & Custom" Grand Lodge of

California - 1926 "*Secrecy is necessary that our candidates may learn and appreciate the lesson masonry teaches. Our Brethren are bound together by this secrecy just as two persons who share a secret are bound together. Secret teachings do not become commonplace. If our lessons are given to the novice with the spice of curiosity they are more readily learned. As mysteries, they have the power to goad men into action but as mere ceremonies known to all, they would soon become worthless. Our imaginations are captivated by anything that is difficult to acquire but anything easily obtained is considered worthless.*"

- Part of the ritual instructs the Freemason "*never attempt to extort or otherwise unduly obtain the secrets of a superior degree*" nor to pass the secrets of his level down to any lower Masonic level "*any more than I would to the uninstructed and popular world who are not Masons*" thereby maintaining a strict system of secrecy within the Lodge.

- "*The order is a semi-secret, semi-public institution; secret in respect of its activities, but otherwise of full public notoriety, with its doors open to any applicant for admission who is of ordinary good character and repute.*" W. L. Wilmshurst, "The Meaning of Masonry", 1927.

- "*The Oriental method of cultivating knowledge has always differed diametrically from that pursued in the West during the growth of modern sciences. Whilst Europe has investigated Nature as publicly as possible, every step being discussed with utmost freedom, and every fresh fact acquired circulated at once for the benefit of all, Asiatic science has been studied secretly and its conquests jealously guarded*'. "The Secret Doctrine of the Rosicrucians", 1949

- "*The Craft represents the unconscious by a body of material which is said to be a 'secret'. As the Candidate advances in Masonic rank - symbolising progressive psychological development these 'secrets' are revealed in the successive Degrees which represent the insights into the unconscious which are characteristic of the maturing individual*'. W. Kirk MacNaulty, "Freemasonry - A Journey through Ritual & Symbol", 1991.

- "*There is a sacred science, and for thousands of years countless inquisitive people have sought in vain to penetrate its 'secrets'. It is as if they attempted to dig a hole in the sea with an axe. Those who profess to reveal the esoterism of such teachings are charlatans. They may try to explain the implication of a certain word or formula as with a conventional secret, but with regard to sacred science, they will never be able to do more than put one word in place of another, and at best this will be bad literature replacing a simple idea*'. Lubicz, "Esoterism & Symbol", 1985

- "*The 'secret' of Masonry is completely indefinable and will always be inexplicable to the uninstructed outside world because it can only be obtained by those who come of their own free will and accord, properly prepared and humbly soliciting. And the knowledge that this humility has been shared by everyone else in the room is the cement which binds Masons. The 'secret' is the shared experience and the presence of even one non-Mason who has not shared that experience would be enough to lose that cement completely"*. Canon Tydeman quoted in Martin Short.

- Freemasonry is *"not a secret organisation but rather has a respectable inclination to privacy"*. Cdr M Higham, Grand Lodge Secretary, referenced in a parliamentary debate, 28th June 1988, during an unsuccessful attempt to outlaw Freemasonry in the Police.

- *"Masonry is not a secret society, it is just that Masons do not reveal their compelling and memorable rituals because this would spoil the fun for those coming after"*, quote from a Masonic contributor to Martin Short.

- *"This hang-up on secrecy seems to come up time and time again, and I simply can't understand why. Our meetings are private, yes, and outsiders are not allowed in, yes, but so what? If we choose to meet behind closed doors, and maintain our silence about what we do, whose business is it but our own? Everything you need to know is in print and even available here on the Internet. Those who wish to know can find out. We have nothing to hide, but we do have things we wish to keep to ourselves which is, as I understand the law of the land, our right as Americans."* Internet Newsgroup - alt.freemasonry.

- *"The greatest secret in Freemasonry is that we have few secrets. A password, a handshake. Our meetings are closed because they are where we conduct our business. Am I permitted in a business meeting of a company I have no affiliation with? Of* course not... Just as I am not permitted in such a meeting, non-Masons are not allowed in our meeting because it is OUR business, not theirs." alt.freemasonry.

- "There are no secrets in masonry! Any "secret" can be found at a medium size library. But beware... Many secrets which are revealed and explained by non-masons are incorrect in content and meaning. The secrets are thought to be secret by a few masons who joined and looked no further. Many anti-masons will hold out secrets which are not masonic in origin and simply not true." alt.freemasonry.

- "One of the many misconceptions of Masonry is not distinguishing between when something is secretive or simply quiet. Our membership is on the decline because of too much silence, truth! But our bad press is typically from narrow sighted individuals who would rather believe rumours than search for information themselves." alt.freemasonry.

- "So many people have written books and leaked things that they are in the public domain. We firmly maintain that they remain secret, although we recognise that in practice they don't. The rest is private in the sense that any club has privacy: you don't let the public into committee meetings of your golf club". Lord Farnham, Pro Grand Master, United Grand Lodge of England, Daily Express 13/5/1995.

- "We have to come out and explain ourselves" but "the secret ceremonies - the history, the handshake, the oaths - are indispensable to our bonding. Members will feel threatened if this is revealed". Jim

Daniel, Grand Secretary, United Grand Lodge of England, Human Resources Magazine, August 2001.

- Martin Short - "*The big secret of Freemasonry seems to revolve around the movement's ultimate goal, elusive and obfuscated as that is*".

There are also some rather mundane reasons why it might suit an individual Mason to keep their activities secret.

- For some henpecked husbands, Freemasonry provides the only safe retreat. It is a corner of their lives that they can keep to themselves. The loyalty they feel towards their fellow Masons and the fear of punishment associated with giving the secrets away is a stronger force than the most bullying wife.

- The ceremonies include aspects, that when viewed out of context by an outsider would be the subject of much ridicule and the Freemason would be extremely embarrassed.

- Some Freemasons just prefer to keep their membership secret since non-members are likely to want to know more about the Craft and as the member is prevented from divulging too much, keeping quiet avoids these awkward situations.

- There is also the boyish aspect of being part of a club that others are not, with the outsiders kept in the dark about what happens inside.

- There are also Masonic "games" such as using words and phrases from the ritual during ordinary conversations, speeches and during business meetings. Non-Masons would not detect these but other Masons on hearing this would use an opportunity to respond with some other words or phrases buried in normal language that would signal to the other Freemasons that "I'm a Freemason as well". The 1975 film, starring Sean Connery and Michael Caine, "The Man Who Would be King" which was based on a story by Rudyard Kipling (a Mason), contains many examples of this type of communication. The same information is conveyed through handshakes, innocently looking lapel badges and particular postures and gestures. Whilst the obsession with secrecy is said to protect the Freemasons privileges and heritage, it also acts as a very effective smokescreen against criticism and independent analysis.

Occasionally though, some argue against it, such as Nelson Hart (Past Grand Master of the Grand Lodge of Canada and a former chairman of the Grand Lodge Committee on Masonic Education) who in 1943 made the point that too much secrecy about the Craft prevented worthy citizens from coming forward as candidates (Transactions of Q.C. Lodge 1974).

However, provided one knows the right people, it is not that difficult to join a Masonic Lodge. Despite the fact that "*an elementary and formal secrecy is requisite as a practical precaution against the intrusion of improper persons and for preventing profanation*", untrustworthy persons have been initiated in every age and exposures of the "secrets" have been published ever since Freemasonry started recruiting members, the earliest known document, as mentioned above, dating from 1725.

Freemasonry has not been unduly affected by these various

exposures and the revealing of the secrets to the outside world has done very little harm, in fact, Freemasonry is more widespread and stronger today than it has ever been. Therefore, it follows that either there are no real secrets at all and that the obligation to keep them private is basically a test of a man's character and loyalty or, as I argue, there are some fundamental facts about Freemasonry which have been cleverly preserved and concealed from ordinary Freemasons (and as a consequence the general public) since open knowledge of this information could destabilise the whole institution as it would mean that very few men would want to put themselves forward as new members.

4) The Initiation

Most members of the public are aware that candidates for initiation are blindfolded as part of the ceremony. This is explained in "The Hidden Life In Freemasonry", 1926, as follows:-

"The candidate is blindfolded for the obvious reason that he shall not see the Lodge or any of its decorations or arrangements till he has taken the solemn Oath on no account to reveal them to any outsider. Until the Oath is taken the candidate is at liberty to withdraw. There have been cases in which the candidate objected to the form of the Oath offered to him and declined to proceed further. In such rare instances he may honourably be permitted to withdraw, and he will be conducted from the Lodge still blindfolded so that no question can arise of his disclosing anything that should be kept secret."

It therefore follows that everything experienced by the blindfolded candidate up to and including the Oath, is not protected by this veil of secrecy. This provides an opening for an inquisitive Mason to start analysing and unravelling some of the mystery without breaking any of the oaths he may have taken and without invoking the usual conditioned responses of avoidance and fear.

It used to be a basic requirement of Freemasonry that you had to ask to join of your own accord rather than be invited in by an existing member. If one were to telephone the Head Office of English Freemasonry in Gt. Queen Street in London and ask to join, you will be told that you should ask someone you personally know, who is a Freemason, that you wish to join. If you do not happen to know any Freemasons then you cannot get in. In practice, however, one is invited by such an invitation as "*If you were to ask me to invite you into Freemasonry, I would be happy to personally recommend you.*"

The subject of recruiting for members will be examined in more detail later, but it would seem that in order to boost recruitment, existing members were officially encouraged in 1981 to solicit for new members. From "Information for the Guidance of Members of the Craft", 1987, "*There is no objection to a neutrally worded approach being made to a man who is considered a suitable candidate for Freemasonry. There can be no objection to his being reminded, once, that the approach was made. The potential candidate should then be left to make his own decision, without further solicitation.*"

What is a suitable candidate for Freemasonry? To answer this it is necessary to understand the process from invitation to initiation that can take well over a year.

The Invitation

The Candidate usually receives a verbal invitation from a friend or business colleague. He is flattered to be approached and has heard that it could help in business even though officially denied. He is likely to be aware that his friend enjoys Freemasonry and sees the opportunity of a new social scene. He knows that it has something to do with charity and is also keen to find out what the fuss is about secrets. He has probably read books and seen TV programmes that suggest that Freemasons have some sort of hidden advantage in business deals and possibly in dealings with the Police and this in itself can be an attraction even though the intention of the original publications was to have an opposite effect.

From the inviting Brothers' perspective, it is his duty as a member of his Lodge is to look for "suitable" candidates. He will look for someone who will readily accept the authority of others and mix in well socially. His candidate will be able to afford the various fees and donations and will be in a position to meet the various time commitments.

As mentioned before, candidates can withdraw from the ceremony up to the point of the Oath, but anyone that is thought likely to withdraw and not complete the initiation, would not obviously be invited.

The inviting Brother will know the extent of enquiry into his candidate's character and there are a number of stages at which his candidate could be rejected. One of the most embarrassing and insulting things that could happen to a Brother is that his candidate should be rejected. It is also very embarrassing for the group that have to make this decision particularly if the recommending Brother is a senior member. Therefore, the Brother would not invite in anyone who might not be accepted by the rest of the group.

The Brother will complete an application form where he has to comment on the candidate's character and also to find another Brother in the Lodge to act as a seconder.

The Visit

Sometime after the application form has been submitted to the Secretary of the Lodge, at least 2 senior members of the Lodge will visit the potential candidate in his home. One of the first questions they will ask is whether he believes in God. It is only important to the visitors that the applicant SAYS he does. He is then asked his motives for wishing to join. (The fact that his friend asked him to join rather than the other way round is forgotten by now). The applicant will make sure that he does not say anything that might indicate that he hopes it will help him in business. He is more likely to say that he wishes to join because of its charitable links.

If the candidate is married, the visitors will request his wife to be present. They require the wife to acknowledge as well as the candidate, that there are annual membership fees to be paid as well as charitable donations. Also that Freemasonry requires weekly attendance at classes of instruction in addition to monthly or quarterly Lodge meetings. The wife is asked whether she consents to this. She usually agrees as she is also under the impression that it might help her husband in business and open up a new social scene.

The visitors use the opportunity to look at the home from the point of assessing the applicant's affluence and any other pointers to whether this man is a suitable candidate.

The visitors seem very knowledgeable and authoritative and the applicant wonders why certain questions have been asked of him. What he does not realise is that the visitors have had to learn what questions to ask and if this is the first such visit they have made, then they are probably as nervous as the applicant.

The applicant is told that the visitors will be reporting back to the Lodge Committee and if his application is successful at this stage he will be required to attend a Lodge committee meeting where other members will have the opportunity to examine him.

The end result of the visit is that the applicant hopes that the visitors recommend him and that the Lodge committee invite him to attend the next stage.

The Committee Interview

After some time, perhaps a few months, the applicant will receive a letter or telephone call from the Secretary of the Lodge stating that he is pleased to inform the applicant that his application has passed to the next stage and that he is invited to attend an interview panel consisting of all the Past Masters and Officers of the Lodge. This sounds awesome but the applicant is comforted to know that his Proposer and Seconder will also be there.

At the interview, the applicant waits in an ante-room while the Proposer and Seconder make their representations to the committee as to why their applicant should be accepted. The applicant is called in and the Master of the Lodge asks again whether the applicant believes in God and what his motives are for wishing to join.

Other questions are asked of him such as whether he has ever been bankrupt and he is asked to acknowledge again that Freemasonry requires time and financial commitments.

The applicant is told that the Committee will consider his application and let him know the outcome in due course. The applicant leaves, hoping that he has not said anything that might jeopardise his chances of gaining membership. He is by now getting very keen on becoming a member.

Sometime later he will receive a letter or telephone call from the Secretary informing him that the Committee have approved his application which will next be considered by the whole Lodge. He will be informed of the outcome in due course.

The Lodge Ballot

Part of the business of the Lodge as distinct from the ritual is to consider applications for membership. The Secretary will read out the application forms and state who are the Proposers and Seconders. The applicants occupation will be mentioned as well as his home and business address. There are two sections to the ballot box and the Brethren vote by placing a voting ball in one of the two sections. If there should be two or more balls in the "no" side then the applicant would be rejected (blackballed). However this would be tantamount to saying that the Brethren had no confidence in the Proposer, Seconder, the visiting committee and the Lodge Committee of Past Masters. It is therefore a rare occurrence that this might happen.

The Secretary communicates with the applicant that he is pleased to inform him that now the whole Lodge has approved his application and just the last hurdle, that of the initiation ceremony, is all that is required of him to get through in order to become a member of the Lodge.

Whereas in the beginning it might have been his friend who suggested that he should join Freemasonry and he did not necessarily feel very strongly about it, by now, the applicant is very keen and excited about becoming a member but the idea of an initiation ceremony will probably fill him with some apprehension. If questioned, his friend will refuse to disclose any details about the initiation with the explanation that the Oath prevents from so doing and in any case it would spoil what would otherwise be a unique experience. It is more likely though, that the member would be fearful that his candidate might abandon his plans to join if he were to find out anything about what was really in store for him.

We can therefore see that a form of preparation has taken

place and that the candidate for initiation has to some extent been conditioned into wanting to become a member. If a candidate gets to this stage, it is unlikely that he will fail to complete the initiation.

The Initiation Ceremony

On the day of the initiation, the Candidate for Initiation (a title which implies that there is a test to pass with the possibility of failure) is brought to the Lodge and waits outside nervously, while the Lodge members take their place in the Temple. As the Brethren pass, they wish the candidate luck and tell him not to worry. This adds to the candidate's anxiety.

One member (the Junior Deacon) will introduce himself and explain to the candidate that he will be looking after him during the ceremony, and provided that the candidate follows and copies him, then everything will be all right. The candidate feels reassured.

The candidate is led to a side room where he meets the Tyler. As well as guarding the Temple from intruders, the Tyler's job is to prepare the candidate for the initiation ceremony. This involves adjusting the candidates clothing and replacing a shoe with a loose fitting slipper. The candidate feels very uncomfortable, exposed and embarrassed. He also feels very awkward as the slipper causes him to limp and shuffle. He is then blindfolded ("hoodwinked" in Masonic jargon). Something that feels like a rope is put around his neck.

The Tyler knocks on the door, and after quite some time, the door is opened and a voice inquires "who is there?" The Tyler responds in a loud voice with the candidate listening intently, "A poor candidate in a state of darkness, who has been well recommended, comes of his own free will and accord, properly prepared and humbly solicits to be admitted to the mysteries and privileges of Freemasonry".

"How does he hope to gain those privileges?"

"By the help of God, being free and of good report".

"Halt, while I report to the Worshipful Master" and the candidate hears the door being shut.

In a short while, the door is opened again and the candidate hears a lot of shuffling. There sounds like quite a few people. Something sharp is pressed against his exposed chest. "Do you feel anything?" he is asked. Before he can say anything, he is instructed to answer "yes".

The Candidate recognises the voice of the Junior Deacon who whispers that he is there and that everything will be OK. He leads the candidate in and turns him round. The candidate then hears a loud voice addressing him from many yards away. He is asked to confirm that he is a "free man" and at least 21 years old. Again he is told by the Deacon how to answer.

He is then helped to kneel, while a prayer is recited that calls upon God to help the candidate through the Initiation ceremony. He hears much shuffling and jangling.

The candidate is asked in whom he places his trust in times of danger and the Deacon tells him to answer "In God".

The loud, distant, authoritative voice of the Worshipful Master says that he is pleased with the candidate's answer and tells him to rise and follow his leader safely as God will now be ensuring that no danger will befall him. The Candidate by now is usually very worried.

The candidate then hears some banging sounds from different directions and the distant voice tells the assembled Brethren that the candidate is going to be passed around them to show that he is properly prepared to be made a Freemason. The candidate wonders what "to be made", means.

He is then led by the Deacon on a lengthy walk turning a few times. They stop and he is pushed sideways where his hand is taken and knocked into something a few times. A different loud voice demands to know who the Deacon has with him. The Deacon repeats what the Tyler had announced earlier, "A poor candidate in a state of darkness, who has been well recommended, comes of his own free will and accord, properly prepared and humbly solicits to be admitted to the mysteries and privileges of Freemasonry". "How does he hope to gain those privileges?" "By the help of God, being free and of good report". The candidates hand is taken from the Deacon, raised up high, he is told to "Enter" and his hand is then passed back to the Deacon.

The blindfolded candidate is then led around some more and a different person asks "who is there?" and the same sequence of questions and answers are repeated. The candidate is then swung around again almost losing his balance, and this person informs the Master that the candidate is ready "to be made" a Freemason.

The candidate is then asked some questions by the Worshipful Master speaking loudly in the distance. "*Do you seriously declare on your honour that, unbiased by the improper solicitation of friends against your own inclination, and uninfluenced by mercenary or other unworthy motives, you freely and voluntarily offer yourself a Candidate for the mysteries and privileges of Freemasonry?*". His guide, the Deacon, before the candidate can fully digest the question, orders him loudly "Answer - 'I do'", and the candidate automatically obeys.

In a similar manner, the Master and Deacon get him to agree that he has a "*favourable opinion preconceived of the Institution, a general desire of knowledge, and a sincere wish to render yourself more extensively serviceable to your fellow-creatures*" and also that he "*will steadily persevere through the ceremony of your Initiation, and if once admitted, you will afterwards act and abide by the ancient usages and established customs of the Order*".

The blindfolded candidate is then pushed and pulled along and given some complicated instructions on how to position his feet. The candidate is aware that he is in front of the Worshipful Master when he hears his voice booming down at him from a few feet above. The Master tells him that Freemasonry is "free" and asks whether the candidate is prepared to take the Masonic Oath. The Deacon commands him to answer "I am".

The candidate is then positioned so that he is kneeling on one knee and his foot is moved to a rather awkward position. One hand is placed on a book which he is told is the "Volume of the Sacred Law" and in his other hand he is given a pair of compasses to hold with one of the sharp points touching the skin of his chest. Some more loud banging is heard. The main thing going through the candidates mind is how to maintain his balance in this very awkward position without stabbing himself in the chest.

Bearing in mind that the candidate has been blindfolded for quite some time, has been led around by the Deacon whilst hobbling because of the ill fitting slipper, in a state of partial undress and hearing much shuffling and metallic jangling sounds with everybody speaking unnaturally loud close to his ear, it is not surprising to realise that the candidate is in rather a confused state. The one constant reassurance is his guide, the Deacon, upon whom he has become dependent and has got used to repeating whatever the Deacon has instructed him to say.

When the Master in a commanding voice instructs the candidate to state his name and repeat the following words after him, the candidate automatically obliges. The Oath seems very lengthy and is broken down into short phrases of 5 or 6 words at a time, which by themselves do not seem to make much sense and prevents the candidate from fully appreciating what he is committing himself to. If the candidate hesitates, the Master will repeat the phrase in such a way as to leave the candidate in no doubt that he has to repeat them. The main gist that the candidate is aware of is about the need for secrecy and the severe punishments that he can expect if he were to break this Oath. By having agreed at the outset that he believed in God, he cannot now complain when he has to call upon God to help him keep this oath.

The candidate is then instructed to seal this Oath with his lips on the volume of the sacred law. The Deacon "assists" by pushing the candidates head down towards the book. After this, the blindfold is suddenly removed at the same time as he hears a startling loud crash and as he recovers from being temporarily dazzled, the first thing the candidate sees apart from the imposing figure of the Worshipful Master bearing down wearing strange regalia, is that the Volume of the Sacred Law is in fact the Bible of his own particular faith.

Let us reflect for a few moments on what has happened so far. In the period from the initial invitation up to just before the actual initiation, the candidates' desire to become a member of the fraternity is constantly strengthened by subtle methods of suggestion and persuasion.

During the initiation ceremony itself, the candidate is blindfolded, jostled, disoriented, exposed, confused and usually in fear. In this state, he takes comfort in the Junior Deacon's guidance and willingly does what he is told. He swears the Masonic Oath and then publicly kisses the Bible to further confirm that this is a solemn obligation and not just a serious promise. The impact of this part of the ceremony will stay with the Mason for the rest of his life with him always believing that he took part in these events of his own free will and accord.

At all times though, the other members of the Lodge taking part in the ceremony (including the Master), are completely unaware of the influence that they are having upon the mind of the candidate. They are more concerned that they do not forget any of their own lines and are seen to be delivering a good performance. They all speak loudly as they are addressing each other from a distance and that they should be heard clearly. However, those sitting in the pews watching and enjoying the ceremony will admit that a "good" initiation can be measured by how much nervousness and fear the candidate displays although all members accept the ritual at face value as an illustration of morality through drama and symbolism.

When the secrets are communicated to the candidate, he is puzzled as to why there was so much fuss about them as he cannot see any special meaning or valuable information contained in the odd words and phrases. In his Oath, he agreed never to write down even the slightest trace of any letter, character or figure belonging to the secrets. This does not present a problem to him as he does not think that anyone outside would be the least bit interested anyway. As it turns out, this is one of the most significant aspects of the whole ceremony, the impact of which will not be felt by him for a few years. This will be further explained later.

He is then shown the secret sign of the first degree. This sign is used frequently in the Lodge particularly when saluting those of a higher rank. This sign serves to constantly remind the Brethren as a whole of the gruesome penalty that they can expect should they ever break their Oath. Next he receives his first Masonic apron and is lectured on its apparent origins - "*it is more ancient than the Golden Fleece or Roman Eagle, more honourable than the Star, Garter or any other Order in existence*".

Another dramatic part of the ritual appears on the surface to be a rather harmless illustration of the virtue of Charity. The candidate is told that he will now be tested on his principles by being called upon to exercise the virtue of charity. He receives a lengthy lecture about the poverty and distress of some unfortunate masons and is asked to give what he considers to be a fit amount in order to relieve their suffering. Then in front of the whole Lodge, he is presented with a collection plate on which he is asked to place his contribution. He feels very guilty and embarrassed for a few moments because he realises that the Tyler removed all of his money and valuables from him before the ceremony began. He is also confused because he knows they know this. Before being able to say anything, he is "saved" by the Deacon who asks him to confirm that if he did have any money on him, then he would have given freely and he is prompted to answer in the affirmative. The Deacon offers this explanation to the Master on the candidate's behalf and explains that the candidate "*expresses willingness but pleads inability*". The Master then apologises to the candidate for causing him any embarrassment but congratulates him on "*the motives by which you are activated*". He is told to always remember the time when Freemasonry accepted him in when he was poor and penniless and to always give as much as he can afford when properly called upon by practising "*that virtue you now profess to admire*".

A later part of the ceremony again reminds the candidate of the obligations he has undertaken and requires him to be obedient to the laws and regulations of the Order and to a "*perfect submission to the Worshipful Master and his Wardens*".

After the ceremony, the candidate is pleased (though puzzled) to be warmly congratulated by the members and feels some sense of achievement. At the meal following the ceremony (known as the "Festive Board"), he is seated on the Masters table next to the Master and he feels quite special when a toast is drunk in his honour. The next time he will sit at this table will be when he is Master.

When the other Lodge Officers are congratulated, usually by visiting Masons, on how well they carried out the Initiation ritual, the candidate begins to realise that he was only a part of the ceremony.

When the candidate returns home that evening, he is likely to have his first encounter with someone who wants to know what happens during an initiation - his wife! He will tell her that he has been sworn to secrecy (she half expected that answer) but the truth of the matter is that he is probably too confused and embarrassed to describe to her the things that he allowed to happen to him that evening, such as being blindfolded, partially undressed and being led around holding another man's hand. Not only does he not want to appear foolish he is also surprised at himself. One Masonic "widow" who wrote to Martin Short sums this up as follows: - "*the sad thing is, when you know what it all means, you cannot believe that your husband, who is otherwise sane and logical, can seriously utter such drivel*".

The United Grand Lodge of England's constitution, which is available to the public, explains that there are three degrees in

Freemasonry. The ritual of the first degree is the initiation ceremony which has been partially described. In the ritual leading from the first degree to the second, the candidate is asked to describe the mode of his preparation into Freemasonry. "I was hoodwinked" he answers.

The second and third degrees have similar rituals and both contain a similar Oath taking process except that the traditional penalties become increasingly more severe and bloody. In all cases, the candidate has to pledge that he will steadily persevere through to the end of the ceremony and also pledge under the penalties of his obligations that as well as the previous information he has gained, he will also conceal the additional secrets he is about to learn.

The drama of the third degree is very powerful psychologically. The subject of death and what lies beyond is probably the greatest human fear and by playing on this, the third degree totally locks the candidate into Freemasonry. As before, the other Lodge members only "see" the drama of their mythical master, Hiram Abiff, who allowed himself to be murdered rather than reveal the secrets of Masonry. The story tells that the body of this Master was subsequently found in a shallow grave indicated by a sprig of Acacia. His body was "raised" from this place and subsequently given a decent burial. In the darkened temple, the Candidate is made to act out the death, burial and "raising" of the Master, surrounded by images of coffins, skull and cross bones and funeral music. In this setting, he can experience extreme terror and is finally "made" a Master Mason by being "raised" to the third degree.

Most members regard the three degree ceremonies as the sum total of the ritual of making Freemasons. It will not be until many years later when the candidate eventually becomes the Worshipful Master of his Lodge, and only then if he consciously thinks about it, that it will dawn on him, that perhaps the most important and difficult part of the ritual, is the actual recruitment process that happens long before the initiation ceremony, where the various participants have to learn, without ritual books or formal guidance, how to entice suitable candidates and properly prepare them for their Initiation into Freemasonry.

5) The Workings of the Lodge

The Lodge (a collective term for a specific group of Masons) usually meets in a Temple about 4 or 5 times a year and one of those ceremonies is concerned with the installation of a new Master. The other meetings deal exclusively with the processing of candidates through the three degree ceremonies. A candidate would normally only experience one degree ceremony per Lodge meeting and as there could be other candidates being processed simultaneously, it can take up to 2 years for a candidate to be taken through all 3 degrees. During the time when the candidate hasn't completed the 3 degrees, he has to leave the Lodge room when the Lodge is working in a higher degree than that to which he himself has been admitted.

At the end of each meeting, some formal Lodge business is conducted such as passing resolutions to increase dining fees and the balloting for new members. Visiting senior Freemasons are saluted in order of their seniority. The members then retire from the Temple to partake in a meal which is itself organised along ritualistic lines and is known as "The Festive Board".

At this meal, visiting Grand Officers convey messages from Grand Lodge concerning news of events and policy changes. Ordinary masons' concerns regarding these visitors' intentions were played down in the Assistant Grand Masters address (31/10/95) when he denied that these visitors were either "inspectors" or "spies".

After a few years it begins to dawn on the new Mason that the only thing the Lodge actually does is to process candidates through the 3 degrees. He also notices that the Lodge Officers move up one position each year as the new Worshipful Master gets installed and makes his appointments for the year.

After taking his three degrees and spending some years passively sitting on the sidelines wondering what he's doing there, he gets invited to become a Steward. The main role of the Steward is to serve wine and look after the needs of the other Brethren at the Festive Board. He also has to start learning the ritual. In a few years time he will be participating in the ritual by occupying the most junior office, that of Inner Guard, which will be the first rung of the ladder leading to the Masters chair.

It is not until the candidate has completed all three degrees that he is handed a copy of the Ritual book. However he cannot learn the ritual in isolation. The book has many words left out except for the first letters. It also omits any descriptions of the intricate actions and movements. Therefore the Brethren have to meet regularly (usually weekly in public house club rooms) at what is known as a Lodge of Instruction. This group is managed by a senior member called the Preceptor. His job is to train the Officers (including the Master) as well as bringing on the junior members. Not only are they to remember their lines but to co-ordinate their actions and take appropriate cues from each other.

The Preceptor, a job that carries high status, is appointed annually by the members of the Lodge of Instruction and will be re-appointed if he can produce a high quality of ritualistic performance in the Lodge.

Masons are not allowed to take their ritual books into the Temple and the Preceptor does not like to see them used in the Lodge of Instruction either. The Preceptor carries significant authority and he will chastise the Brethren (including the Master) if they have not learnt their parts. If a Brother gives a poor performance in the Temple, the Preceptor feels let down and the Brethren know that they will incur his wrath.

As mentioned above, the full Lodge only meets a few times a year and it is likely to be working a different degree ceremony each time. Therefore, each Officer only gets one or two opportunities to perform his parts of the different degree rituals in a year before he is moved to the next Office where he plays a different role in the rituals. Therefore there is much pressure upon him to get it right first time. He wants to deliver a good performance so as to set a good example to the junior members, particularly the candidates on the one hand, and to elicit praise from the senior members on the other. He also wants to make a good impression upon visiting Masons, especially those he invited himself as well as the visiting Masonic dignitaries, since the quality of his performance reflects on the standing of his Lodge.

At the Festive Board, the visitors will usually comment if the ritual was carried out in a polished manner and the Brethren that took part will feel proud. If they made any mistakes, they will be privately criticised by senior members and the Preceptor is likely to lecture them at the next Lodge of Instruction meeting.

We can now see the other side of the coin and understand why the Officers have little time to reflect upon the experiences that the candidates are undergoing. As far as the Officers are concerned, it is they themselves that are on display.

The Mystery of the Missing Words

It was mentioned above that many words are left out of the ritual book. This therefore makes it harder for the Mason to learn. Because of the amount that he has to learn, he spends many hours on his own going over and over the ritual, trying to lock it into his memory. Obviously, if he were to write the missing words into his ritual book, life would be easier. However, the Masonic Oath that he took as a candidate, never to write down even the least trace of any character, letter or figure, and that he has heard recited over and over again by other candidates and that he now has to learn himself in order to administer it to the candidates that he has to process, prevents him from doing so. The psychological effect is so strong that the very thought of writing on the ritual book has the same impact as a religious man contemplating defacing a bible.

Hannah, in "Darkness Visible", observed that there are some different versions of the ritual book with slightly different words or phrases. Before the time of printed ritual books, the complete ritual used to be memorised. Probably, in order to counteract the spate of "illegal" printed texts, some authorised versions made their appearance. The different versions of the ritual represented the fact that the ritual had been handed down by word of mouth for a long time. The differences, though, are slight enough that a Mason brought up on one dialect ("working") will not feel out of place in a Lodge that practises a different working.

Hannah noticed that when he compared the different ritual books, different words were omitted from each. For example the explanation of the penal sign of the third degree is given as:

Emulation Ritual - "*The P. S. is given b. d. t. h. s. a. t. b., d. i. t.*

t. s., a. r. w. t. t. t. t.n. This is in allusion to the p. of your Obl., implying that as a man of honour and a M.M., you would rather be s.i.t. than improperly disclose the secrets entrusted to you."

Taylor's Ritual - "*The P.Sn. is given by p. the r.h., t.e. to f. a S., to the l.c. of the b., d.i.s.a., d.i. to the s., and r. on the C. This you will perceive alludes to the penalty of your Obligation wherein you have sworn, that as a man of honour, and a M.M., you would rather be s. in t. than improperly disclose the secrets of the Degree."*

He regarded this as a blunder on the Masons part and used this knowledge to help fill in the gaps and produce his own complete exposure. The point that he missed was that it did not really matter what words were missing just as long as there were words missing.

Masons and non-Masons believe that the missing words are to help keep the ritual secret from prying eyes. Hannah has shown that it is a fairly trivial job to reconstruct the missing words based on their initial letters and the context of the sentences. If it was too hard, then Masons would probably give up trying to learn it. The object of the exercise is to get Masons to repeat the ritual over and over to themselves. (If you see a man apparently talking to himself in his car and he is not using a mobile telephone then he is probably rehearsing his Masonic ritual).

Is there another reason, other than giving a word perfect performance in the Lodge, for this need to constantly rehearse the ritual which is made all the more difficult because of the missing words?

An example from the world of advertising might throw some light on this. Imagine there is a breakfast cereal called "Wheaty Flakes". On the side of the cereal box there is a competition to win a dream holiday. The consumer has to answer a few simple questions or rank some items into order of importance. Nearly everybody that glances at it will notice that they know the answers and the possibility of a dream holiday enters into their consciousness. All of these competitions have a tie breaker question. The fact that it is called a tie breaker implies that you are already a winner apart from one last tiny hurdle. You can almost see yourself on that Caribbean beach.

All you have to do is to supply the missing words to the phrase "I like Wheaty Flakes because...........".

The first few answers that you come up with do not impress you too much, so you think of a few more. Different people stick with this exercise longer than others. Some even go as far as completing the application form and sending it in. Of course someone will win the holiday, usually a professional competition player. However, the objective of the marketeers is to get you to repeat to yourself as many times as possible, "I like Wheaty Flakes", "I like Wheaty Flakes" and this is psychologically linked with visions of palm trees, sunny, empty beaches and deep blue sea.

These methods are not dissimilar to subliminal advertising which is now illegal and statistics show that these type of competitions help maintain brand loyalty. Arnold points out that the principle of repetition has always been at the heart of advertising.

Hannah, and others who "fill in the gaps" and publish the ritual, may actually be helping Freemasonry to keep one of its major secrets buried, since to outsiders the completed texts appear to be rather boring and repetitive mumbo-jumbo and interest in the secret ritual of the Freemasons soon wanes.

Those researchers who do focus on the missing words tend to

limit their enquiries to looking for clues in the origins of the more obscure Masonic words.

The Role of the Master

Provided nothing unusual happens, each Officer will progress up the Masonic ladder automatically until he finds himself installed as Master of the Lodge. This can take up to twenty years from the time he was initiated.

The main function of the Master is to maintain the continuity of the Lodge for the year. Apart from his first task of appointing his Officers (which is basically advancing each one up to the next position) his main focus is on the amount of the ritual he personally has to remember and perform as he is expected to give a flawless performance each time and set an example to the rest of the Lodge. All Masons from Initiates to Master Masons who have not started attending the Classes of Instruction and seen the Master struggling to remember his lines along with everyone else, will tend to hold the Master and his Wardens in awe and assume that they possess some special knowledge.

All the administrative tasks connected with the running of the Lodge are handled by the Lodge Secretary (the only member to have his fees paid for him) and the financial affairs are in the hands of the Treasurer. Order in the Lodge is maintained by the Director of Ceremonies. The Charity Steward collects the charity, the Chaplain leads the prayers and the Almoner is concerned with matters relating to the sick and bereaved. These Officers do not take an active part in the ritual and are drawn from the ranks of the Past Masters and will hold these posts for many years. They make up the Lodge Committee who take all major decisions but it is the Lodge Secretary who might hold his office for 10 or even 20 years, that is the real power behind the "chair". For instance it is he who makes the confidential recommendations to Grand or Provincial Lodge for Brethren to receive higher Masonic honours.

The Master is basically a figurehead whose main task is to learn volumes of ritual and get through his year without any hitches. He happily accepts guidance and direction from the Lodge Secretary. In the same way it is the Grand Secretary who runs the show at Grand Lodge rather than the Grand Master. Short refers to the Grand Secretary as Freemasonry's "Prime Minister" and the Brethren are forbidden to write or communicate with the Grand Master except through the Grand Secretary. As a point of interest, Grand Secretaries used to receive a proportion of the total fees collected by Grand Lodge.

The final ritualistic part that the Master plays at the end of his year is to install the next Master. He then becomes the Immediate Past Master (IPM) for the next year, where his real job is to prompt the new Master should he forget any of his lines. At the end of this next year, the IPM joins the ranks of the Past Masters and sits on the sidelines until he is offered a job such as Almoner or Charity Steward. He could wait for many years. It is at this point that many Freemasons start wondering about Masonry as it begins to dawn on them that as far as the Lodge is concerned, they have played their useful part.

Each year, a Past Master from each Lodge will usually be rewarded with promotion to the next Masonic level. In London this is known as London Grand Rank and in the counties, as Provincial Grand Lodge. These members are selected on the basis of reports submitted by the Lodge Secretary. The promotion is regarded as a special honour and holders are saluted at Lodge meetings and toasts are drunk to their health at the Festive Boards. After many years service at this level, they may be promoted to Grand Lodge and are held in even greater esteem by ordinary members.

From time to time, a group of restless Past Masters, usually from the same Lodge, will get together and apply to Grand Lodge to start a new Lodge. These Lodges are known as "daughter" Lodges to the Lodge in which the members were originally initiated into, which is known as a Brothers "mother" Lodge. There is much kudos in being a founder of a new Lodge. Also, by founding a new Lodge, the Past Masters get an opportunity to take an active part in the ritual again until the "suitable" candidates have been recruited and work their way up the Masonic ladder. Forming a new lodge is also the way to impress the hierarchy and improve the chances of receiving Masonic honours.

The process of Mother Lodges spawning Daughter Lodges is the method by which Freemasonry has managed to survive and grow substantially over the last 200 years with its tentacles reaching every corner of the globe.

Thus the primary function of the workings of the Lodge "machine" is self preservation, continuity and expansion. The fuel for this machine is new candidates. A "suitable" candidate is one who can afford the time and money and will steadily advance through the various degrees and Offices without rocking any boats, eventually occupying the Masters chair for a year and at sometime thereafter, to become involved in founding a new daughter Lodge and thereby replicating the whole process.

Most Masons attitude towards the ritual is that it is something to be endured and a small price to pay relative to the pleasures and benefits they derive from Freemasonry. The fact that they do not take the ritual seriously does not mean that the psychological effects previously mentioned are any less effective. On the contrary, with most Masons thinking about subjects such as the Festive Board menu, these suggestions are able to slip straight into the sub-conscious without the Mason ever stopping to think whether what he is hearing is valid or not.

Guy Arnold ("Brain Wash", 1992) commenting on TV advertising, explains that the advertisers know that even though the appearance of a TV advertisement in the middle of a programme might provide a break to make sandwiches or get a beer from the refrigerator, the conscious mind is still taking note of the ad. He also says that "*to state something as though it is an infallible truth or has been proven beyond doubt is a well-developed technique*".

Another example of this, is that every Initiate is told (and thus every Mason hears repeatedly) that the Masonic apron is more honourable than the Order of the Garter. The fact is, that the Order of the Garter is the highest honour that the reigning monarch can bestow and was established by Edward III in 1348. It is limited to 25 holders at any one time plus the Sovereign and other descendants of George II occasionally appointed. Despite the argument that the meaning of this part of the ritual is not to be taken literally, unless Masons consciously question what they hear, this type of suggestion constantly repeated, takes on the appearance of a fact. Similarly, as mentioned previously, the frequent saluting to each other is a constant sub-conscious reinforcement of the bloody penalties associated with breaking the Masonic Oath.

Arnold points out, "*human beings, have persuaded themselves of their unique qualities and like to think that they are superior to all other living things because of their intellect and powers of reasoning, but curiosity and inventiveness on the one hand are all too often offset on the other by the mental laziness that too readily accepts 'received wisdom' from above and ceases to question those who provide it*".

6) Social & Business

Today it is very common to hear the word "networking". It seemed to catch on as a conscious and targeted activity when people first started using Filofax style organisers to not only to schedule their business appointments but their social engagements as well. Prior to the Filofax, people used to keep diaries but each year they faced the chore of copying out the names and addresses at the back of their diary into next year's one. As the Filofax was a loose leaf system, this enabled the social contacts section to grow and grow as well as more space to enter additional information.

People realised the benefit of building up a large databank of information about people they knew and the new people they met, which could come in handy at some point in the future possibly relating to job opportunities, social events, needing business or trade services, etc.

There were even seminars teaching people how to grow their network, which places to go to network, how to exploit your network and even what networking clubs to join.

With the use of electronic organisers, now a feature on most mobile phones, people were able to store vast amounts of contact information with search facilities so that they could quickly pull up a list of say lawyers in their network that they might want to contact.

The Internet has added a new dimension to social networking (e.g. Facebook and Twitter) and business networking (e.g. Linkedin) where much of the communication is happening instantly.

Freemasonry is probably one of the oldest networking clubs. Before the days of the Internet or other networking channels, Freemasonry provided a useful service to its community in this regard. I can certainly remember tapping into the network when I needed some high quality printing and another time when I needed some advice from a surveyor. You knew that anyone recommended to you was likely to give you a fair price and not rip you off.

Furthermore, if you were travelling abroad on business or vacation, you could, through your Lodge Secretary, get an introduction to the Masonic community in the town or city you were travelling to and where you would be made most welcome.

It is this networking aspect of Freemasonry that draws many men towards it. Lodges particularly welcome member's guests from other Lodges and in return the guest will invite the member back to his Lodge to be his guest. About half those present at a meeting will be guests and therefore there are always new people to meet.

For many others, it was a family tradition with sons of Masons (known as a "Lewis") being able to join when they were 18 years old instead of the minimum age of 21 years for everyone else. When my father suggested to me that it could be beneficial to join, although I was not very enthusiastic, I joined because I didn't think it could do any harm and maybe some good but also as I knew it would give him pleasure sharing this aspect of his life with me.

Others join, not for the network but for the company. Here they can find like-minded men who they can enjoy mixing with a few times a year, sharing a joke and a beer. For some older men, particularly those that are widowed or lonely, Freemasonry can satisfy their social needs. Some Lodges are part of a Masonic Centre where a number of Lodges hold their meetings and to which a social club for all the might be attached, again providing more opportunity for social interaction.

Another source for recruiting Masons is from within the workplace or organisation. Masons often suggest membership to their fellow work colleagues as a way of expanding their business network. Where it might be understood within a particular organisation that being a member could improve promotional prospects, a person might seek out a Mason to propose him for membership. It is commonly thought that within some sections of the Police, that promotion could be more difficult if one was not in the Craft. The fact that there are some police-only Lodges doesn't do much to dispel this myth (if it is a myth).

I recently met with Dominic Torr, author of numerous spy novels including "Hoodwink", a story featuring Russian agents and Freemasonry, but not in the way that Stephen Knight suggested KGB agents used Freemasonry to advance through the ranks in the Civil Service but how some of his characters in the legal profession used the cloak of Masonic secrecy to carry out their deeds and to solicit favours.

He was prompted to write his story after verifying an actual case of a solicitor (a non-mason), who having uncovered some wrongdoing by another solicitor within the firm and reporting this to the senior partner, found himself to be the one fired – all the others were Masons who stuck together and excluded him. After trying to make a go of a legal practice on his own and finding obstacles at every turn, he eventually threw the towel in and reluctantly accepted an invitation to join a Lodge because it was apparent that in his large town with eight Lodges in it, unless he was "on the square" he would not survive in his profession.

Torr's view is that it is the legal profession where Masonic membership is most rife and his enquiries as part of his research for his book led him to believe that participating barristers more easily got regular briefs from solicitors that were also members and that becoming a "silk" was much easier. One QC, not a Mason, often chose as a junior a known Mason to benefit from his members.

Those in the trade professions, like builders, might join because they believe that by being involved it could make their jobs easier such as when they need architects to sign off their work or help with planning permission.

A strong motivator in days past, and maybe less relevant these days, is the use of Freemasonry to overcome class barriers. Not only does one get the opportunity to rub shoulders with those further up the social ladder, but Freemasonry gives the opportunity to any member, irrespective of class, to rise up the Masonic pecking order (to a certain level) so that the local milkman could, in theory, be senior to the Lord of the Manor. Many of these men haven't achieved much in the way of social status in the outside world and Freemasonry can fulfil their need to be recognised as important.

Others are able to develop social skills such as speech making through which they are able to build self confidence. There are also opportunities for sportsmen with inter-Lodge and inter-Province activities. Many golf clubs have their own Masonic Lodge and there are also Masonic bowling, darts, caravan clubs and even a Sub-Aqua Lodge.

For the more technologically minded, there is even an Internet Lodge, where masons the world over can attend virtual lodge meetings in "cyber-space" using the modern working tools of the computer, telephone and router.

Once a year, a Lodge will hold a "Ladies Festival" or "Ladies

Night" which is a dinner and dance basically put on to thank the wives for their tolerance in allowing their men folk away so much. Some find the Ladies Night rather condescending but for most Masons and their wives it is the highlight of the year particularly for the Master since he and his wife are the stars for the evening, sitting on the top table making speeches and having toasts drunk in their honour.

Even those wives that are distressed by the time, money and secrecy that their husbands devote to the Craft will usually put their concerns aside to appear to fully support their husband all the more so during "his year" as Worshipful Master.

However it is also the Masters responsibility to set up and co-ordinate a Ladies Festival committee. They will arrange the hall, music and catering. The number of guests will be estimated and the total cost divided by this number will generate the cost per ticket. Each Master wishes to host a more elaborate affair than his predecessor - one that the members will talk about for years to come. Each member of the Lodge is expected to purchase a ticket for himself and wife and also to invite (and pay for) some guests, especially those he is planning to recruit into the Lodge. The Master is expected to invite and pay for many guests. A well attended Ladies Festival is a measure of the popularity of the Master whereas a poorly attended function that makes a financial loss has to be personally made up from the Masters own pocket. This can run into many thousands of pounds and is obviously a very stressful time for a Master. If a Ladies Festival should make a profit though, this is taken into Lodge funds. While the Master is having sleepless nights, the other members are looking forward to enjoying themselves.

Some Brethren take their Masonic seniority very seriously and enjoy being waited on and respected by the junior members. If he has a particularly high rank, he will be accorded much courtesy when he visits other Lodges, be invited to sit on the Masters table and will be the recipient of many toasts and salutes. To make it near to the top in Freemasonry such as Provincial Grand Master is the goal of many, although few will actually achieve it. Martin Short has analysed the social rankings of the Masonic hierarchy and concluded that the highest any "commoner" can hope to aspire to is Senior Grand Deacon, and only then if the person is someone with wealth and worldly status.

Knight and Lomas ("The Hiram Key") point out that once the succession of lords of the realm started occupying the senior positions, the sorts of common men who had been early Grand Masters never held that office again. Neither did they take the position of Deputy Grand Master which was taken by nobles of lesser ranks, who carried out the Grand Masters' administrative work.

Those that do achieve the lofty heights will rub shoulders with nobility and royalty and have very active social calendars being invited to every Lodge meeting and function in their province. Obviously, they cannot attend every meeting and have to be selective. The Lodges selected to receive these senior Brethren feel very honoured but sometimes they were simply chosen because they had an interesting menu.

"Badger", a Masonic contributor to Martin Short, found that above a certain Masonic level, the rich and influential people were highly indiscreet in conversation amongst themselves although probably as not as indiscreet as a John Ward (born 1885) who referred to the Masonic masses as *"dumb and inarticulate brothers, often never hoped for Grand Lodge honours, but quietly did their duty in maintaining the grand fundamental principles of our order"*. It was obvious to "Badger" that Masonic promotion did not depend on merit and ability but on patronage and privilege. If you have a lot of money to dish out to the Charity, you are well on your way to Provincial and Grand honours. "Badger" sees Freemasonry as a mechanism of social control and that by drawing in people like police officers, lawyers, local government officials and businessmen, the landed aristocracy and big business filter their values down through the social structure, and at the same time draw in these groups so that they can be controlled and used.

The British, as well as being very secretive about their incomes, are also very discreet about their Masonic membership, and very few, if any, list their Masonic membership in "Who's Who", unlike their overseas brethren who proudly list their Masonic rank alongside their other social distinctions in the "International Year Book and Statesmen's Who's Who". Some examples from the 1968 version are:

- Mr. WWK - Mason 33 deg;

- Mr. EGK - Past Master, A.F. & A.M., Member and Past Officer, Royal Arch Masons, Knight Templar;

- Mr. HL - Brotherhood of Free Masons, Scottish Rite, Mystic Shrine;

- Mr. AMM - Masons, Toronto; Island Chapter No. 1, Royal Arch Masons, Havana, Cuba;

- Mr. FSM - Past Grand Master United Grand Lodge of N.S.W.1947-49, past G.M. Mark Masons of N.S.W. 1946-48, Inspector-General Rose Croix Masons 33 deg.

However, the American Masons were not as welcoming to all races as the British. According to the Time-Life book, "Ancient Wisdom and Secret Sects", 1989, where John Hamill (Grand Lodge Librarian) was the consultant on the Masonic content,

American blacks are usually excluded from white lodges. Those that wish to become involved with Masonry, usually join the Prince Hall order.

This evolved out of a lodge that was started in 1775 by fourteen "men of colour" in Massachusetts and was called the African Lodge of which Mr Prince Hall was its first master.

It was struck off the roll of Grand Lodge of England in about 1800 for falling into arrears. It tried to re-establish links but was denied access perhaps because of the race issue which is clearly explained by the Grand Chaplain of the Grand Lodge of Massachusetts in 1795 who is quoted as saying *"white Masons, who are not more skilled in geometry (Freemasonry) than their black brethren, will not acknowledge them....the truth is they are ashamed of being on an equality with blacks"*. As a result of this attitude, the African Lodge declared its independence from Grand Lodge.

Today there are more than 5000 Prince Hall lodges with over 300,000 members. After 200 years, the Grand Lodge of England in December 1994 finally recognised the Prince Hall Grand Lodge of Massachusetts again, although the Grand Secretary reminded the brethren that they were still banned from having dealings with other Prince Hall lodges for the time being.

By March 1996, Grand Lodge had still only recognised the Massachusetts "Prince Hall" Grand Lodge. In North America 14 Grand Lodges had by this time recognised and allowed reciprocal intervisiting with Prince Hall Grand Lodges not recognised by Grand Lodge of England, and because of this, English brethren were banned from attending Masonic meetings in many states including California and Colorado. English Masons were also advised that brethren from these US states were not welcomed at English lodge meetings (Prince

Hall - latest update).

Freemasonry can also influence international social relations. Not too long ago, English Freemasons were instructed not to fraternise with their German Brethren because the Germans were maintaining Masonic links with French Freemasons who were not recognised by Grand Lodge. Sometime after, the Germans broke off their Masonic links with the French and the English were once again allowed to visit German Lodges.

In 1991, Grand Lodge withdrew recognition of the Grand Lodge of India. In December 1995, discussions were still continuing as to how relations with India might be restored. Greece had been out of bounds for masons since 1993 and although the Grand Lodges of England and Greece had appeared to resolve their differences by June 1996, English masons were still barred from visiting until the Greek suspension was formally lifted.

The Sunday Times (27th June 1993 - "Masons to shun mafia brothers") reported that Grand Lodge had instructed English Masons not to visit Italian Lodges because of problems of corruption, organised crime and mafia violence. This followed alarm among Masonic leaders that their Italian Brethren were out of control.

In September 1993, Grand Lodge broke off relations with the main Italian Masonic body, "The Grand Orient of Italy", after reports of "illegal Lodges, unregistered Brethren, links with other unrecognised and irregular Grand Lodges and interference by other Masonic orders". An alternative Italian Grand Lodge which was started in April 1993 called "The Regular Grand Lodge of Italy", recruited its members from the discredited Grand Orient. It applied to the Grand Lodge of England for recognition, reporting "that its members are all men of good character and uninvolved in Italy's current scandals". Recognition was granted in December 1993 on the basis that if it were denied, it "might encourage other Grand Lodges in Italy to attempt to fill the vacuum".

Freemasonry in Business

During the Initiation ceremony the candidate is asked to declare on his honour that he voluntarily offers himself as a candidate, uninfluenced by mercenary or other unworthy motives. Apart from disputing whether he does anything voluntarily, most Masons will privately admit that they joined Freemasonry because they believed it might help them in business or with career prospects.

The public perception about secret business advantages can actually generate applications from such minded persons. The business connection manifests itself in a number of ways. Firstly, the fact that most Lodges are restricted to about 70 members means they get to know each other very well. In the same way that members of say a golf club, church or local political party might do business with each other because they know each other, the same is true of the Lodge. They might as well let a friend have their business instead of a stranger and conversely they are likely to get a better price from a Brother than an outsider.

Secondly, in social situations, men quickly establish whether the person they are being introduced to is a Mason through the handshake which is then qualified by some verbal exchanges, undetectable to the non-Masonic ear, and this enables them to break the ice and establish a relationship very quickly. If the subject of business comes up and they discover that their mutual business needs can be met by each other, because of the Masonic connection they are likely to be predisposed to working with each other. A typical scenario is that one will invite the other to his Lodge and then vice versa following which not only might they do business together but so will other members of their respective Lodges.

Thirdly, and this is the grey area, is where men who meet in business situations discover that each other are Masons. If the men represent themselves in business then it is entirely their own affair with whom they do business. But where they represent their employers in contractual situations such as buying or selling or negotiating contracts then their Masonic allegiance could influence their decision making (not necessarily to their employers benefit) without the subject of Freemasonry ever being mentioned.

Do Freemasons get preference over non-Freemasons in job interviews and promotions? On the one hand there is the aspect of helping a friend which can obviously occur in many ways such as tipping him off when a vacancy comes up or offering a trainee position to his son, etc. The other type of situation is where men meet in, say, an interview situation and discover that each other are "on the square". Most Masons will confirm that they would not give preference to the Mason per-se, but where two candidates are evenly matched, then Masonic membership might swing it in his favour. The justification would be that the Mason shares the same moralistic beliefs and therefore he's probably a decent chap whereas the other applicant is an unknown quantity.

There are other aspects to the interview situation which are less obvious. If the interviewer carries a more senior Masonic rank than the interviewee, then he knows that his Masonic authority will carry some weight in the work situation in addition to his managerial authority. He knows that the junior Mason will work just that bit harder and is unlikely to be a troublemaker. Part of the "Ancient Charges" emphasises that *"All Masons employed shall meekly receive their wages without murmuring or mutiny, and shall not desert the Master till the work be finished'*. The junior Freemason will always believe his Masonic link worked in his favour when in reality it could have worked against him.

This can also be a problem where a junior employee can carry a more senior rank than say his manager or even his Managing Director. Does the junior employee get the perks or does he actually miss out so the manager cannot be accused of favouritism?

One of the other negative aspects to Freemasonry in the work place is that it provides the opportunity for rumour-mongering and disharmony amongst non-Masonic employees. Beliefs about the unfairness of certain decisions such as promotions or golden handshakes being tied to a Masonic link can cause severe morale problems in the work force.

And it is not only male non-members that often feel discriminated against in business but professional women in particular, who being fully aware of the "glass ceiling" might also be coming up against "blue walls".

Freemasonry as a Business

In the chapter on Other Degrees and Orders, I explain that each degree has its own set of regalia, ritual books and lodge furniture which has to be purchased from a specialist store. The main supplier of these items is a firm called Toye, Kenning & Spencer of Great Queen Street, London, situated directly opposite the Grand Lodge.

Interestingly they were founded in 1685, some 30 years before the creation of Grand Lodge. I am reminded of the time old puzzle – what came first, the chicken or the egg?

The Master Masons Handbook of 1894 contains no less than

15 pages of advertisements for Masonic paraphernalia all available from George Kenning of Great Queen Street, London. The list includes, 40 different books and publications, about 30 Masonic music scores (including "The Freemason; or, Tell me the sign, John"), calendars, subscriptions to the Masonic newspaper "The Freemason" (also available from all "good" newsagents), menu cards, summonses and programmes, guest cards for Masonic balls and parties, banners, jewels, clothing, furniture, Masonic candles and Tracing Boards.

As Masonic Lodges multiplied, Brother Kenning obviously had a very lucrative trade supplying Masonic clothing and furniture for all of the lodges and members working the various degrees and ceremonies. As each new Masonic Order was created, this brought another wave of customers through their doors. This business has been a very successful enterprise for hundreds of years. Not only was there a huge captured and expanding market with repeat orders every time a Brother took another degree, but the Brethren could hardly shop around for the best prices. Below is a table of prices from 1894.

Degree	Fee	Cost of Clothing		
	£ s. d.	£ s. d.	to	£ s. d.
Craft	5 5 0	0 8 6	-	0 15 0
Royal Arch	2 2 0	1 15 6	-	3 17 6
Mark	2 2 0	0 18 0	-	1 7 6
Royal Ark Mariner	1 1 0	1 0 0	-	1 7 6
Royal & Select Masters	2 2 0	0 7 6	-	0 12 6
Allied Masonic Degrees	2 2 0	1 10 0	-	2 10 0
Royal Order of Scotland	5 5 0		-	4 9 6
A. and A. Rite, 18°	5 5 0	6 6 0	-	9 4 6
A. and A. Rite, 30°	10 10 0		-	7 9 6
A. and A. Rite, 31°	10 10 0		-	9 15 0
A. and A. Rite, 32°	10 10 0		-	10 0 0
A. and A. Rite, 33°	11 11 0		-	11 0 0
Knight Templar	3 3 0	5 18 0	-	7 9 6
Knight of Malta	1 1 0	2 5 0	-	2 11 0
Red Cross Constantine	1 1 0	2 0 0	-	2 6 0
K.H.S	0 5 0	0 15 0	-	1 1 0
Rosicrucian	1 1 0	0 15 0	-	1 1 0
Secret Monitor, 1°	1 1 0	0 7 6	-	0 12 6
Secret Monitor, 2°	0 10 6	0 7 6	-	0 12 6

Furniture and Appointments

for Craft Lodges, from £30 to £100;

for Royal Arch Chapters, from £50 to £150;

for Mark Lodges, from £30 to £40;

for Red Cross of Rome and Constantine, £30 to £50;

for Knights Templar Preceptories, from £30 to £50;

for Rose Croix Chapters, from £30 to £50;

for Secret Monitor Conclaves, £12 12s.

A sign of the times though is that even the catalogue retail stores, recognising the size of the market and the sales opportunities, now offer a range of Masonic jewellery, including a ring where the "swivel top hides secret symbol".

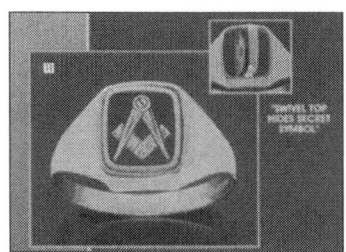

Masonic book publishing is another lucrative business. In 1886, Lewis Masonic was established, specialising in the publication of Masonic texts. Then called A Lewis, the focus of the company was exclusively on ritual books from Masonic Craft degrees through to the Masonic side orders. In 2005, they started selling some of the non-secret texts such as Masonic speech making and historical theories, through regular high street book stores.

Martin Faulks, first decided to join Freemasonry after reading a book called "The Hiram Key" by Christopher Knight and Robert Lomas, published in 1996. A few years later he landed the Marketing Manager's job at Lewis Masonic.

As part of his plan to launch Lewis Masonic to the outside world, he persuaded Robert Lomas to write a new book for the occasion. "Turning the Hiram Key" was published by Lewis Masonic in 2006 and Faulks not only got a mention inside the book but also had his picture on the front cover in one edition and proudly announced on his blog that he was now famous.

In one promotional interview, Faulks even claimed that some

Freemasons thought that Lomas might be the inspiration for the character of Dr. Robert Langdon, in Dan Brown's thriller, The Da Vinci Code. In 2007, Lewis published another Lomas book "Turning the Templar Key" and Faulks was given the honour or writing the Foreword.

With responsibility for commissioning and promoting titles, it is noted that Faulks' wife, Philippa, an author in her own right, in 2009 published through Lewis Masonic her own book called "A Handbook for the Freemason's Wife".

Even Lomas takes the opportunity for a bit of family business. The last page of "Turning the Hiram Key" advertises some Masonic jewellery. The advert says "*Masonic truths are traditionally illustrated by symbols, so Robert sketched his symbol of the Hiram Key which represents his truth and feelings about Masonry. Jewellery designer Delyth then created a beautiful sterling silver tie-pin to bring this symbol to life*".

The advert continues that the tie-pin can be bought by mail order from Delyth Jewellery or from their website as well as the full range of Delyth's Masonic jewellery being available internationally from website www.thefreemason.com and in the shops of Toye, Kenning and Spencer. What Lomas doesn't tell us is that Delyth, the jewellery designer, is actually his daughter Delyth Lomas.

7) Masonic Charity

Charity is one of the basic principles of Freemasonry which has supposedly been concerned with the relief of distressed Freemasons, their families and dependants from the very beginnings of the Order. Soon after the creation of Grand Lodge, the charities were centralised in 1727 when all lodges were "called over" to pay their lodge's contributions into the Charity Fund.

Most candidates state that their main reason for joining Freemasonry is so that they can be part of a charitable organisation and "do their bit" for society. On the other hand there have been many members and their families that through some misfortune in life, have found themselves in a position where they have to solicit assistance from the Masonic charities. Provided they can show that they are on low enough incomes, they can take advantage of subsidised private education for their children and retirement homes for the elderly.

The charities are all run by committees of Past Masters and those men that enjoy committee work are drawn down this route. There are many opportunities to serve on committees that are concerned with judging the requests for financial assistance from those members or their families that have fallen on hard times.

Apart from many locally run Masonic charities, there are three main centrally organised charities. These are the Grand Charity (concerned with helping needy Freemasons and their dependants and more recently some non-Masonic charities such as the Royal National Lifeboat Institution where the

Grand Master in 1980 presented a lifeboat to himself as President of the RNLI), The Masonic Trust for Boys & Girls (whose object is to relieve poverty and to advance the education of the children of Freemasons) and the Masonic Foundation for the Aged and Sick (which acts as fund raising body on behalf of elderly and sick Freemasons and their dependants).

As a point of interest, the Rickmansworth Masonic School used to be part of the Royal Masonic Institution for Girls but in 1978 became an Independent School but it is still obliged to take girls placed there by the Trust.

When one studies the history of Freemasonry it is interesting to see the role that charity played. In 1717, four London Lodges came together and formed the first Grand Lodge. Soon there were other Grand Lodges with those of the "Antients" and the "Moderns" being bitter rivals. The Royal Masonic Institution for Girls, founded in 1788 by Bartholomew Ruspini was recognised and supported by the Moderns Grand Lodge. In 1798, William Burwood, Past Master of the United Mariners Lodge on the roll of the Antients, instituted the "Masonic Charity for Clothing and Educating the Sons of Indigent Freemasons".

In 1813 the two rival Grand Lodges buried their differences and came together as the United Grand Lodge. However, while the Antients admitted children of both branches of the fraternity to its school, the Moderns refused to admit the daughters of the Antients until a Special Court in 1815 ruled otherwise.

The first Masonic charity for the elderly was called "The Asylum for Aged and Decayed Freemasons" and came into existence in 1835. However, the then Grand Master, H.R.H the Duke of Sussex withheld his official support and in fact instigated a rival charity in 1842 known as "The Royal

Masonic Benevolent Annuity Fund".

Apart from the 3 main Masonic charities in existence today there is also the Royal Masonic Benevolent Institution (which runs residential homes for elderly Freemasons and their widows), the Royal Masonic Hospital (which used to exist primarily to treat Freemasons and their dependants), and the Masonic Housing Association (which builds sheltered housing mainly for elderly Masons). These charities are managed by over 100 Past Masters, many of whom are personally appointed by the Grand Master.

There are still serious disputes today regarding the Charities and Short provides a detailed account of the bitter internal dispute regarding the Royal Masonic Hospital and the split between the "sell" and "no sell" camps which culminated in the current Grand Master, the Duke of Kent, together with Prince Michael of Kent (Grand Master of Mark Masons) withdrawing their support from the Royal Masonic Hospital (Daily Telegraph 30/11/91). In September 1985, Viscount Chelsea, President of the Foundation of the Aged and the Sick pledged "if the hospital tried to remain open the foundation will starve it of funds". He seems to have got his way because in an attempt to channel funds into a new charity called the "New Masonic Samaritan Fund", an address by the Grand Master in April 1993 and circulated to all Brethren, instructed them to stop collecting for the Hospital - "*Given the pressure on the Crafts charitable resources, and the need to avoid making excessive demands on them, it would be wrong to permit the Hospital to appeal to the Craft for funds*". In a letter from Grand Lodge to all Masons dated 8th December 1993, they were informed that an attempt by the Hospital to raise funds by selling competition tickets should be ignored as "*leave has not been granted for this venture*". The hospital closed soon.

How do these formal Charities relate to the individual mason who has joined the fraternity?

As mentioned previously, the first the new candidate hears about charity is during the initiation ceremony. Sometime after the Oath has been sworn, the candidate is given a lecture by the Master on the virtues of charity. He is then asked for his contribution.

However, as part of the preparations for the ceremony, he had all his money and valuables removed along with some of his clothing. He therefore feels a bit embarrassed that he is unable to give anything. The Master explains that there was no attempt to sport with his feelings, rather to impress upon him that if an opportunity arises for him to practise charity to a Brother in need he will remember the time he was accepted into Freemasonry poor and penniless.

The first opportunity comes at the end of his first meeting when the charity box (the charity column) is passed around for donations. The Charity Steward, a Past Master and thus carrying much authority, will make himself known to the new Brother and explain to him his charity obligations. He is expected to give as much as he can afford, preferably by way of a covenant (minimum period four years) to the current Masters chosen charity, which is always one of the main Masonic charities. (Masters can in fact choose any charity they like but if it isn't one of the recognised Masonic charities, the Masonic hierarchy will not only frown upon it but the Lodge might find that none of their members will receive Masonic honours for many years).

In the 1994 issue of the New Masonic Samaritan Fund Newsletter, the Fund's President acknowledged the influence of the initiation ceremony on initiates and observers in relation to the giving of charity "*We all remember the day when we were received into Masonry. If we were in a bit of a haze during the ceremony, we are frequently reminded as we watch others joining, of the pledge we made when it was explained to us that the distinguishing characteristic of a Freemason's heart is Charity".*

The popularity of a Master is measured by the amount of charity collected from the Brethren of the Lodge and with a spirit of competition he encourages the members to give more than they gave to the previous Master.

The Charity Steward being personally appointed by the Master, expresses his loyalty by being as successful as he can in collecting as much as possible and he will approach each member at every meeting clutching his list of who's given what.

The standing of a Lodge in a Province (outside London, Lodges are part of a Province which roughly correlates to a county, and are ruled by Provincial Grand Lodge, which in turn is ruled by Grand Lodge) is measured by the amount of charity that the Lodge has collected as compared to the other Lodges in the Province which is published in league tables.

Each year, each of the three main Charities will have a particular Province assigned to collecting for it and this is known as a Provincial Festival. The published programme allocating Provinces to charities goes well into the 21st century.

The Provincial Grand Master has the responsibility for collecting for his assigned charity and usually, the Masters of the Lodges in the Province will select their Provincial Grand Masters' charity as the one they are supporting in their year as a mark of respect for the Provincial Grand Master.

The Provincial Grand Master will usually start collecting for his charity several years before his Festival. The Festival itself is a dinner to celebrate the culmination of the appeal, attended by many distinguished Brethren from the Grand Lodge plus those Masters and their wives that are committed enough to purchase tickets. The total amount raised will be announced and the Provincial Grand Master will hope to raise more than his counterparts in other Provinces.

In addition to the Masters List, other money for charity is collected during the meals following the Lodge meetings to which the visitors also contribute. Often a distinguished visitor from the Provincial or Grand Lodge will address the Brethren at the meal on the need for enthusiastically supporting Masonic charities in general and the Provincial Grand Masters preferred one in particular.

Each Lodge produces Lodge accounts each year that are audited and circulated to the Brethren. However, the amount of charity that the charity steward collects on behalf of the Master is not published since it is a private matter between the Brother concerned and the steward.

During Festival years, members contributing more than a certain amount will be awarded a medal (a "jewel"), which if the Grand Master approves, can be worn at all Masonic functions and meetings. Many members give just in order to receive the medal which they proudly wear. The Assistant Grand Master in his October 1994 address stated "*I am basically not in favour of charity jewels but I do acknowledge their usefulness in raising money*". In case any of the brethren in the audience were unable to read between the lines, he went on to say "*to make it easier to acquire the jewel, a desk has been set up outside for when you leave*".

As a Past Master, to be selected to work on any of the Charities Management Committees is regarded as a high honour and it is often felt amongst the ordinary Brethren that those who have given the most support (money) to the Masonic charities seem to be the ones selected.

Calculations as to how many hundreds of thousands of subscribing Masons there are and guesses as to the average amount of annual Masonic charity donations they make, one is likely to arrive at a figure for the total income in terms of tens of millions of pounds. The published figures for the amount of grants and donations awarded to non-Masonic Charities amounts to less than 1 million pounds and are believed by some to be just a PR exercise. How the rest of the money is utilised should be openly disclosed to the brethren by Grand Lodge.

The cause of charity has also been used fraudulently against the gullible Freemason. The ancient charges state with reference to a stranger declaring himself to be a Mason in need "*you are cautiously to examine him in such a method as prudence shall direct you, that you may not be imposed upon by an ignorant, false pretender, whom you are to reject with contempt and derision, but if you discover him to be a true and genuine Brother, you are to respect him accordingly; and if he is in want you must relieve him if you can.*"

Because of the above passage, many Masons fall victim to fraudsters. The 1890 Master Masons Handbook warns "*The young Mason is invariably picked out as the prey of numerous unscrupulous adventurers. Some, unfortunately, really Masons, who degrade the Craft into a means of gaining a livelihood; others, mere impostors, who have accidentally got hold of some chance word or phrase, generally quite inaccurate, on which they trade. Our newly-raised Brother must remember that he is only enjoined to give such relief to the worthy distressed Brother as he can do without injury to himself or connections, and by giving indiscriminately to every beggar he only promotes the imposture on other Brethren."*

Just as Freemasonry spread around the globe, so did this aspect of charitable abuse. The 1926 publication "Masonic Law and Custom" produced by the Grand Lodge of California states that "*Most Masonic frauds stop the individual mason on the street and try to get money from him. The first thing for the inexperienced mason to do is to suggest that the applicant go to the nearest Master or other officer of the Lodge. The Master is authorised to dispense relief for the Lodge. You have no such authority. Due to his position and his greater experience, he is better qualified to extend the assistance needed and to avoid cheats. If you are not in a position to send the applicant to a Board of Relief or a Lodge, you may satisfy yourself so far as is possible that he is in good standing and if necessary get him a room for the night, and food, but be wary about giving him cash.*"

Freemasonry strives to maintain its public image as a charitable organisation and by implication, that its members are charitable by nature and devoted to this cause, whereas the reality is that charity is the price Masons have to pay to justify their continued membership and to keep the Charity Steward at bay. If they were really in it for the charity, they could just as easily satisfy this requirement from outside the Lodge.

As well as the centralised Masonic charities, Lodges often maintain their own charity funds. Grand Lodge has been advising the Lodges since 1986 to place their charity funds with the Grand Charity for ease of administration. The Quarterly Communications of Grand Lodge published in September 1994, reports that the number of participant lodges has increased from 1500 to 2350 in the previous twelve months. This element of the Grand Charity currently stands at about £10 million.

The rule book of the Grand Charity is titled "The Constitutions and Regulations of the Grand Charity of, but not under, the United Grand Lodge of England". The reader's attention is drawn to the words "of, but not under", a point we shall return to later. The Members of the Grand Charity are selected from members of Grand Lodge with the Grand Master being *ex officio* the Grand President of the Charity and the Grand Secretary, being the Secretary of the Charity. Most Masons are unaware that apart from any charitable donations they may make, part of their annual lodge membership fee is also channelled to Grand Lodge which collects this money on behalf of the Grand Charity, thereby assuring it of a healthy income each year.

The Fund of the Grand Charity is managed by a company called "Masonic Charity Trustee Limited" which was incorporated in 1980. The Board of five Directors includes the Grand Secretary, who is also the Company Secretary. At least one other has been a Grand Secretary with another being a Grand Scribe. The objects of the company include acting as executor of wills and administrators of the estates of deceased persons. It is also authorised to *"engage, employ and remunerate such staffs and such professional or expert advisors as may be necessary for, and conducive to, the attainment of the objects of the Company"*. Those expert advisors did not do so well in 2002 when the Grand Charity Annual Report November 2002 admitted that 'Speculative' Masons lost £3.8 million pounds on the stock market.

"Badger" (in Short) relates a story of when he visited a high ranking Mason to congratulate him on his involvement in establishing a well appointed and luxurious retirement home for elderly Masons or their widows who he assumed could ordinarily not afford such fees. It was made clear to the shocked "Badger" that only those that could afford the full fees were welcome and preferably only those that had no dependants so that they would leave their money to Freemasonry when they died. Is this the reason behind Masonic Charity Trustee Ltd's main object of acting as executor of wills?

The practice of individual charity was once a basic principle of Freemasonry operating at local level, but today the centralised Masonic Charities seem to exert such an influence upon Freemasonry that the spirit of charity is used as a mechanism of control.

8) Origins & History

The origins of Freemasonry are, apparently, a mystery. This fact alone has caused tremendous interest and over 50,000 books, pamphlets and articles have been written trying to establish the origins and purpose of Freemasonry.

Many members derive satisfaction from researching the history of Freemasonry. The "prize" of solving this mystery has led many Masons to devote a lifetime of study to this subject and there are constantly new theories being published.

The Quatuor Coronati Lodge in London (The Premier Lodge of Masonic Research) was founded in 1884 by nine eminent Masonic scholars for the purpose of intellectual study of all facets of Freemasonry. Their style of research shunned the baseless conclusions that had been derived from the imaginative writing of earlier authors. Through their efforts, the work of Masonic historians of the previous century came under close scrutiny and much that had been blindly accepted in Masonic lore was rejected.

One of the main mistakes that many writers made was to mix up the origin of the ritual with the beginnings of the order. Trying to develop a direct line from ancient Egypt to the Grand Lodge of England has taken many on a wild goose chase.

One example from "The Essene Odyssey" by Hugh Schonfield, states that between "*400 BC to 200 AD Egypt had become the melting pot of the ancient world. On the foundations of its ancient faith had been superimposed superstructures introduced by alien rulers, Medo-Persian, Greek and Roman while there had been an increasingly strong Jewish influence. As a consequence there were religious fusions and amalgamations that lent their characteristics to Jewish Essenic teaching and found a Greek expression in the Hermetic and Christian Gnostic. The coverage of the Roman Empire right round the Mediterranean carried the cults with it. Another wave would sweep across with the later advances of militant Islam. Thus the mystical secret societies of Europe could and did look back to Egypt as their ancestral home. The Rosicrucians could look back to an Essene impetus from Egypt relating to matters associated with King Solomon, creator of the Temple, which was also the foundations of Freemasonry."*

R A Schwaller de Lubicz in "The Temple in Man: Sacred Architecture and the Perfect Man" tells how he spent 15 years on-site at the Luxor Temple in Egypt. He measured the entire temple, including every block and inscription, and proved that the plan of the temple was rigorously based upon human proportions and designed to symbolically represent man. Each detail of masonry and symbolic art expresses an element of the Egyptians' comprehensive knowledge of man's physical and spiritual anatomy. The human being embodied in the geometry of the temple's architecture is meant to represent Pharaoh, symbol of the Perfect Man.

A common theme is to draw a line from the builders of the Temple to the medieval stone-masons who built the cathedrals and were formed into Guilds. Secret passwords and other modes of recognition were allegedly used by these travelling stone-masons in order to prove their level of skill and thus their level of wages. Some researchers have pointed to the fact that Freestone was a common building material of that time and that this might be the origin of the name Free-mason. It is then argued by many, that some members of the gentry were permitted to join these guilds, possibly to boost funds. These non-operative stone-masons were apparently initiated and took part in the secret rituals which had been preserved since Egyptian times. These were known as "speculative" masons. The theory is that in time, enough non-operative masons had joined these Guilds and then they broke away and formed the Speculative Masonic Lodges of today.

"Born in Blood, The Lost Secrets of Freemasonry" by John Robinson, 1989, points out the unlikely aspects of this theory particularly questioning why the medieval stone-masons would have such barbaric punishments associated with giving away their secrets.

Robinson's' theory (like many before him) suggests that the origins lie with the warrior monks known as the Knights Templar who were founded in 1118 and explains that in 1307 they suffered arrest and persecution by Pope Clement V at the behest of King Philip IV of France who wanted to acquire their wealth. The English King (Edward II) was reluctant to enforce the Papal Bull and a delay of 3 months allowed the Templars to escape to England and go underground and become a secret society. Robinson maps their progress up to 1717 when he claims that the political situation was such that Freemasonry felt safe enough to declare itself to the world and go public with the founding of the Grand Lodge.

In order to bridge the gap between the romantic theory of the Knights Templar and today's Freemason, Robinson concludes that with Freemasonry losing its original reason for existence it became simply an over-indulgent eating and drinking club. He believes the leadership had to find a new sense of purpose and they decided that Masonic Charity should be the main focus. Baigent and Leigh in "The Temple and the Lodge", 1989, also promote the Knights Templar link.

Others believe that Masonry evolved out of the Rosicrucians, another secret society, which has a ritual based around alchemy, in the same way that Masonic ritual uses stone masons tools. It is believed that the Rosicrucians were formed in 1610 and was based on the mythical figure of a certain Christian Rosenkreutz, a German nobleman who had donned the robes of a certain order of monks and visited India, Persia and Arabia and had returned bringing with him a certain Secret Doctrine obtained from the sages and seers of those Oriental lands. He was said to have established the original Rosicrucian Brotherhood about 1425.

Pythagoras (582-500 BC) features in both Masonic and Rosicrucian writings. In 529 BC, he founded a "Brotherhood bound by vows of sobriety and self control and to the observance of certain mystical rites". Pythagoras was the first to teach that the earth was a globe, found the relationship between the length of a musical string and its pitch and also taught that numbers held the answer to the meaning of life. His school also discovered "irrational" numbers through attempting to find the square root of 2 although they tried to conceal this discovery as they could not explain it satisfactorily.

Pythagoras' theorem relating to right-angled triangles is depicted on the regalia of a Past Master. Clarke, writing in the Transactions of Quatuor Coronati Lodge, volume 87, points out that the knowledge of the 3:4:5 right angled triangle was used to construct the Temple at Jerusalem and the Pyramids. Also, that the Society of Operative Masons holds as fact that the three principle characters of Masonic lore had in their possession, rods of these particular lengths. The correct use of these rods was a jealously guarded and valuable secret. King Solomon's was 5 units long, Hiram, King of Tyre's 4 units and Hiram Abiff's was 3 units. Thus, a right angled triangle, fundamental to building work, could not be constructed by any one of the three without the consent and co-operation of the other two. When Hiram Abiff was killed his rod was lost and it was the exact length of this rod that had to be re-discovered before work could be resumed.

Magus Incognito in the "Secret Doctrine of The Rosicrucians", 1949, states that Pythagoras gained his mystical knowledge from the Egyptians and Persians and it is believed that through him it passed to the Grecians. He also says that it is possible that the Egyptian occult school was an offshoot of an original and older Teaching which had its origin in the lost continent of Atlantis.

Grand Lodges' official position is that Freemasonry is one of the world's oldest societies of men, whose main purpose is the teaching of moral and spiritual values and the practice of charity. As mentioned earlier, the Grand Lodge was created in 1717 by four London Lodges uniting together. The earliest known Lodge dates from 1621 and another from 1646. The first was the Acception Lodge attached to the London Masons Company and this connection is probably the reason for belief that Freemasonry evolved out of the guilds of stone-masons. The second reference is based on the diaries of Elias Ashmole who stated that he was initiated into Freemasonry in Warrington in 1646 but according to Masonic researcher, A C F Jackson, there is no evidence of an actual Lodge in Warrington at that time.

It would seem that the newly formed Grand Lodge set about destroying or covering up evidence of the existence of earlier Lodges in order to establish its own position as the only Masonic authority. Robinson states that in 1718, one year after it was formed, Grand Lodge instructed all Lodges in England to hand over any documents or ancient records in their possession, ostensibly to assist Grand Lodge in drafting a constitution.

Apparently, many Lodges resisted this attempt by the Grand

Lodge to assert its authority and reacted by burning their documents.

Grand Lodge also set about altering the ritual to suit its own ends. For instance, Martin Short points out that the mythical master, Hiram Abiff, did not appear in the ritual until 1720 and he suspects Dr John Anderson (author and copyright owner of first Grand Lodge Constitutions) as the inventor of the legend. Even senior Mason, Eric Ward, believes that Freemasonry was created independent of the building trade and that the ritual was made up. "*This ritual did not have to be old, but it needed to appear so, and most importantly an element of secrecy had to be embodied.*" Short agrees "*all the evidence indicates that the rituals worked today with sadistic oaths were invented by Freemasonry's eighteenth century masters who found the genuine oaths too tame for their purposes*". Knight and Lomas ("The Hiram Key", 1996) though still maintain Hiram Abiff did exist in the person of Seqenenre Tao, an Egyptian King whose mummified body in the Cairo Museum shows injuries to the head similar to those described in the ritual.

From the lack of evidence prior to the 1600's it seems quite likely that Freemasonry started sometime around then rather than the notion that they had been in existence for hundreds or indeed thousands of years prior, meeting in totally secrecy and completely unknown to the world.

It was certainly the case in England during the 1600's that if a group of like minded individuals got together to follow their own religious beliefs that was at variance with the established church, they would have to conduct their affairs in secret since England was in a state of religious persecution. Christopher Hill in "The Century of Revolution 1603 - 1714", 1980, points out that in 1629 Parliament passed resolutions that anyone who introduced "innovation of religion" should be regarded as "a capital enemy to the kingdom and commonwealth". Everyone had to attend services in his parish church every Sunday and was liable to legal penalties if he did not.

This was also a period of severe taxation. The Crown introduced many schemes for raising finance including the selling of titles and monopolies mainly to fund their various wars. There were no safe investments in England under the government. Hill recounts a story from 1640 when the government seized £130,000 bullion which private merchants had placed in the Tower of London for safety, causing numerous bankruptcies.

Asa Briggs in "A Social History of England", 1983, quotes Richard Overton from 1646: "*What will not all oppressed, rich and religious people do to be delivered from all kinds of oppression, both spiritual and temporal, and to be restored to purity and freedom in religion, and to the just liberty of their persons and estates?*"

The same book quotes Sir Simonds D'Ewes: "*All our liberties were now at one dash utterly ruined if the King might at his pleasure lay what unlimited taxes he pleased on his subjects, and then imprison them when they refused to pay. What should freemen differ from the ancient bondsmen and villeins of England if their estates be subject of arbitrary taxes?*"

It was also the case that the State had no interest in the relief of the poor. The Poor Law was aimed at providing sufficient employment to prevent disorder. Relief of poverty was left mainly to the private initiatives of wealthy merchants and tradesmen. Between 1601 and 1660 they voluntarily contributed over £1,000,000 to various schemes for relieving poverty which by today's standards would be equivalent to about 1.5 billion pounds (measuringworth.com). Over this same period, the nobility, by contrast, donated less than £75,000.

A brief review of English history, in relation to religion, during this period, provides a background against which to chart the emergence of Freemasonry from being an unknown secret society to a semi-public organisation.

In 1603 the Crowns of England and Scotland were united in the person of James Stuart, VI of Scotland, I of England. The accession of James I was seen by both Puritan and Catholic dissidents as an opportunity to try and win concessions they had long wanted under Elizabeth I and the outlines and language of the religious argument that was to persist throughout the century, began to emerge in the first decade. At the Hampton Court Conference of January 1604, unfortunately the King and Puritans failed to agree.

When James was about to become King of England, Thomas Percy (steward to the Earl of Northumberland), had been sent by the English Catholics to Scotland to ascertain how he was disposed to deal with them. James, then in a mood to promise anything likely to help him to his wishes, gave his word that he would tolerate the Mass, albeit "in a corner". Percy and those who sent him were completely deceived, and Percy in consequence thirsted for vengeance. Percy became one of the Gunpowder Plot conspirators.

The architect of the Gunpowder Plot was Robert Catesby, "a gentleman of family and fortune". He had been a supporter of the Earl of Essex who had promised liberty of conscience. This promise was broken and the incensed Catesby adopted the "bloody and unscrupulous project of blowing up the King, Lords, and Commons at one blow". Others who embraced his scheme included Guy Fawkes, Thomas Winter and Francis Tresham.

Typical of the treatment that Catholics were receiving at that time was the story of a Mr Pound, an elderly Catholic gentleman from Cheshire who complained to James on behalf of his co-religionists that they were being unfairly treated. James's response was to have Pound taken to Fleet Prison where he was nailed by his ears to the pillory and fined a thousand pounds. As Catholic priests were being hunted down, fines were multiplying daily against those that had any connection with them. It was known that "the sword of the law was about to receive a keener edge in the next parliament".

It is believed that Francis Tresham in warning his Catholic Brother-in-law, Lord Mounteagle, not to be present in the Upper House on the date of the planned gunpowder event, let the cat out of the bag and hence Guy Fawkes was apprehended.

Following the failed scheme of 5th November 1605, laws inflicting every conceivable kind of injury and humiliation on the Catholics were passed by immense majorities. A day of thanksgiving was officially celebrated.

James died in March 1625 and his son became King Charles I. In 1626, writing and preaching about controversial matters in religion was prohibited. Charles I is quoted as saying that "people are governed by the pulpit more than the sword in times of peace". "Religion it is that keeps the subjects in obedience" was typical of the attitude.

In 1629, Charles I dissolved Parliament and started raising money by fines imposed by the Star Chamber, illegal taxation and the selling of monopolies. 1630 saw the introduction of Distraint of Knighthood, an extortionate method by which English gentry were forced to contribute large sums to the Crown.

1646, as well as the year of Elias Ashmole's initiation at Warrington was also the year in which Oliver Cromwell defeated the Royal forces of Charles I and ended the Civil War. In 1653 Oliver Cromwell became Lord Protector and died in 1658. His son, Richard, took over this mantle, but in 1660 Parliament restored the throne to the royal line by inviting Charles I's son to ascend the throne which he did as Charles II.

In 1661, Parliament passed the new Act of Uniformity which ushered in an era of persecution for all who could or would not accept the doctrine and constitution of the Established Church in particular the doctrine of "Passive Obedience". 1662 saw the Quakers Act introduced which imposed severe penalties for Quakers meeting for worship.

1673 saw Charles II issue the "Declaration of Indulgence" which released the Puritan Dissenters and Roman Catholics from the penalties attached to nonconformity. Parliament however, strongly opposed this and Charles withdrew it but it gave rise to the Test Act of 1673 whereby every man who held any office was compelled to subscribe to the essential doctrines of the Church of England.

In 1689 the Toleration Act was passed that allowed all non-conformists except Unitarians freedom of worship and although they were denied their full religious and civil freedom, they avoided the strong prejudices and penal laws that continued to affect the Roman Catholics.

During this period there was also a lot of interest in the supernatural and mystical with groups such as the Rosicrucians forming. MacNaulty tells us "*it seems certain that those who wished to pursue an interest in the Hermetic/Kabbalistic traditions had to exercise the utmost discretion*".

1693 was the beginning of Britain's National Debt when William borrowed £1 million at 10% interest to pay for war with France. In 1694 the Bank of England was founded in order to manage the public debt.

As the 17th century drew to a close the threat of religious persecution for non-conformists receded and this apparently enabled the secret Masons to relax a little for although they would claim not to be a religion they would almost certainly be regarded by outsiders to be non-conformists. However, various Acts were passed against the non-conformists such as the Schism Act of 1714 which was aimed at restoring the Church's educational monopoly and destroying the non-conformists schools.

Other events of this period provide pointers to the nature of society at that time. In 1712, a tax on newspapers and pamphlets was introduced aimed at reducing popular discussion amongst the lower levels of society. Witches were still being tried with the last executions taking place about this time. The Royal Africa Company lost its monopoly in exporting slaves to Jamaica which caused this trade to substantially increase with over 42,000 slaves being delivered to Jamaica in seven years. This was also the era of the South Sea Bubble fiasco when many thousands of first time investors suffered financial ruin with suspicions being laid at the door of George I's court. According to a Dr Plumb, this was a time when "*without protection, the poor, the weak, and the sick went under; the rich and the strong prospered*".

It was against this background that in 1717, four London Lodges joined forces and created the Grand Lodge, effectively publicly announcing their existence to the outside world, although John Hamill, Grand Lodge Librarian, comments in his book, "The Craft", 1986, that this event was completely ignored by the press of the day. Hamill's book, written to counteract the negative effect of Stephen Knight's attack on Freemasonry, tells us that no records of the four founding lodges exist and also that no minutes were kept of the first six years of Grand Lodge's existence.

"*By forming a Grand Lodge under the control of an elected Grand Master, the four Lodges had effectively set up a control system for Masonry which ensured that only they were exempt from its dictates but all other Masons had to conform to its edicts*" (Knight and Lomas, "The Hiram Key" 1996).

Very little is known about the first Grand Master, Anthony Sayer, but it was the second Grand Master (1718), George Payne, an official of the Commission for Taxes, who compiled the first Grand Lodge regulations. From this point on, Grand Lodge began to initiate new regulations and to administer the newly created centralised Charity Fund. It also started to rapidly export Freemasonry around the globe, getting into countries such as Spain, France, Holland and Belgium in the early 1720's, Gibraltar and India in 1728, the East Indies in 1729 and North America in 1730.

In 1768 it sought a Charter of Incorporation which would enable it to purchase property. A Bill of Incorporation was presented to Parliament but it did not reach its third reading, it being feared that this was a legal device to misappropriate the Charity Fund for other purposes.

During the 1700's, there was a significant growth in the number of Lodges. The qualification for membership as defined in the Ancient Charges was, "*good and true men, free-born, and of mature and discreet age and sound judgement, no bondsmen, no women, no immoral or scandalous men, but of good report*". This is further qualified since no Brother can be made a fellow-craft (second degree) unless "*he is also nobly born, or a gentleman of his best fashion, or some eminent scholar, or some curious architect, or other artist descended of honest parents*".

Rival Grand Lodges were formed:- the Antients Grand Lodge in 1751, the Grand Lodge of All England in 1761 and the Grand Lodge South of the River Trent in 1778.

According to Stewart in his introduction to the 1987 edition of Hutchinson's 1775 book "The Spirit of Masonry", the Craft appeared to have lost a much needed "sense of direction" for nearly one quarter of the Lodges had stopped meeting by the 1760's and had consequently closed down.

"*Membership of the Moderns' Lodges* (as the Grand Lodge became known) *needed to be increased, especially as the rival Antients were better organised and were attracting and retaining increasing members. Hutchinson's book* (sanctioned by Grand Lodge) *may have been intended to attract more and better educated men who had more than a passing interest in the Craft as merely just another club.*"

"*Freemasonry was widely and almost constantly ridiculed in the popular press. The general tenor of the required additions* (made by Grand Lodge to Hutchinson's book before they approved its publication) *was an attempt to demonstrate ancient origins and therefore social acceptability by reference to classical and biblical literature and to ancient history.*"

"*No doubt the continuing conflict with the Antients' Grand Lodge was a factor in persuading Petre* (Lord Petre was the then Grand Master) *to try to counter their opponents' more organised system of Lodges by assisting recruitment to membership of Lodges nationwide.*" Thus it appears that Grand Lodge initially encouraged claims for biblical and ancient historical origins in order to boost recruitment.

The 1700's was a popular time for starting new secret

societies, all of which relieved their gullible members of joining fees and promised salvation or enlightenment of some kind. This was becoming such a problem that in the 1790's a number of Acts were passed in Parliament against oath taking and secret societies. An Unlawful Societies Act was passed in 1799 to outlaw these groups, however, somehow Freemasonry managed to be specifically exempted from the terms of the Act.

The recruitment drives continued and in 1813, the two rival Grand Lodges amalgamated and called themselves "The United Grand Lodge of Antient Free and Accepted Masons of England" and its development since then has been well documented elsewhere.

Royalty became very much involved from the earliest days of Grand Lodge, eventually taking over the leadership of the organisation. *"The higher echelons of the Craft were slowly taken over by the royal family who sought to maintain their influence in the most republican organisation in the world'* (Knight, C. and Lomas, R. "The Hiram Key" 1996).

The first known royal Freemason was Frederick Lewis (Louis), Prince of Wales, who was initiated in 1737 by his chaplain, Rev John Desaguliers, who was the 3rd Grand Master. This was the same year that he was dismissed from Court by his father, George II, who wrote in a letter to his son *"such contempt for my authority and of the natural right belonging to your parents cannot be excused by the pretended innocence of your intentions, nor palliated or disguised by specious words only. The whole tenor of your conduct for a considerable time, has been so entirely void of all real duty to me that I have long had reason to be highly offended by you'*. His mother who had referred to him as "that villain" also wrote of him *"My dear first born is the greatest ass, and the greatest liar, and the greatest canaille, and the greatest beast in the whole world, and I most heartily wish him out of it"*. In "King George III" by John Brooke, 1972 in which the current HRH Prince of Wales writes a foreword, Frederick is variously described as "undutiful to his parents, unfaithful to his mistresses and disloyal to his friends", "insincere, indifferent to truth and really childish", and "not an able politician or man of resolute mind". He seems hardly the ideal role model for a Freemason. Nicknamed "Poor Fred", he became a Master of a lodge one year after his initiation in 1738 and had a town in Virginia, USA, named after him (Fredericksburg, scene of a famous battle in the American civil war). He never came to the throne since he predeceased his father, apparently dying from a cricket ball injury in 1751, but his eldest son became King George III. In 1752, George Washington was initiated into Freemasonry in the Fredericksburg Masonic Lodge.

At least six Kings as well as numerous princes have been Freemasons although in accordance with the precedent set by King George IV, royal princes resign from active participation in Freemasonry on ascending the throne.

King George VI was particularly involved. He was initiated into the Naval Lodge No. 2612 in December 1919. In 1922 he was appointed Senior Grand Warden of the Grand Lodge of England, and in 1924 was made Provincial Grand Master for Middlesex. He was invested and installed by his great uncle, H.R.H. the Duke of Connaught. He held the latter position until he ascended the throne in 1938. As King, he accepted the rank of Past Grand Master of the United Grand Lodge of England, and was ceremonially installed at the Albert Hall in London before an audience of Masons from all parts of the world. In 1935 he accepted and was installed Grand Master Mason of Scotland, and affiliated with the Lodge of Glamis, No. 99, Scotland, where his father-in-law, the Earl of Strathmore, was a Past Master. He was a Royal Arch Mason and was a First Principal. He was a Past Grand Master of the

Mark Lodge and former Ruler of the Mark Province of Middlesex (1931-37). He held the rank of Past Grand Master, and of Knight Commander of the Temple, was a 33rd Degree, and Grand Inspector General in the Ancient and Accepted Rite of Rose Croix.

The royal association is formally acknowledged in the initiation ritual where a candidate is informed about the high standing of the body that he has just joined "*and to so high an eminence has its credit been advanced that in every age monarchs themselves have been promoters of the art, have not thought it derogatory to their dignity to exchange the sceptre for the trowel, have patronised our mysteries and joined in our assemblies*". The ritual also demands that the Mason should "*never lose sight of the allegiance due to the Sovereign of your native land*".

In chapter 6 we touched on how Masonry can have an international influence and one wonders whether this was the main reason behind Royalty taking over the leadership of Freemasonry. During the expansion of the British Empire, Masonry could have played a significant role since senior Freemasons visiting foreign lands often established Lodges in those countries. The Lodges would recruit members of the local ruling class, so it was not too long before there was a significant number of influential people in those countries that had sworn the Masonic Oath and by implication allegiance to the Grand Master and hence the British Monarchy. In fact, Knight and Lomas believe that the linking between Freemasonry and Royalty has been the main reason for the survival of the British Monarchy.

Robinson in "Born in Blood" describes how the Knights Templar gained their power through initially setting up an underground international communications network. The Masonic communication channels could have proved equally useful to the Monarchy. In this respect it is interesting to note the George VI's 3d stamp which is the only British stamp to feature Masonic symbols. This stamp was issued on 11th June 1946, and was known as the Victory Commemoration Issue. According to the Stanley Gibbons catalogue, the 3d stamp symbolised Peace and Reconstruction. To the general public this stamp would not raise much curiosity being part of a set featuring industrial images but to Masons world-wide in receipt of a letter bearing this stamp, it would be very significant – the 3d stamp was only used for postage to foreign lands.

The stamp can be interpreted on a number of different levels. As far as the general public were concerned, the dove with olive branch represents peace, the trowel and brick wall rebuilding and the square and compasses planning for the future. At another level, a Mason would be reminded of his Oaths by the Square and Compasses, his allegiance to the Sovereign by the Trowel (see reference above) and the twig could represent the Sprig of Acacia symbolising the death of the Hiram Abiff who gave his life in order to preserve the Masonic secrets. Other Masons might notice that the particular position of the Square and Compasses indicates a Fellow Craft while the Trowel can be found on the Charity Steward's regalia and the Dove with Olive Branch on the Deacon's regalia. The dove and olive branch also features in the Mark Masons degrees. Was the stamp to remind the

Brethren of their allegiance to the Crown or some sort of secret recognition of their part in the war?

In a similar manner, the Dollar bill, as well as carrying the portrait of George Washington who was initiated into Masonry in 1752 but refused to be Grand Master of USA, also features the Masonic "All Seeing Eye" which matches that depicted on the Grand Masters jewel which is a reminder to Masons that the Great Architect is watching them. Conspiracy theories have been circulating in the US since the early 1800's implying that Freemasons control the economy through the manipulation of paper money and persons who embrace this view often point to the Masonic symbols on the Dollar bill as evidence of this conspiracy.

"All Seeing Eye" on the Grand Master's Jewel

"All Seeing Eye" on the Dollar Bill

Much of this view stems from the creation of the Anti-Masonic Party in 1826 in the United States which was incidentally the first American third political party. This party was founded upon public indignation and suspicion of Freemasons which was ignited by the disappearance of William Morgan who was apparently preparing a book revealing the organisations secrets. Anti-Masonic candidates were successful in many state and local elections and various anti-Masonic newspapers flourished. In 1831, the party held a national convention and nominated William Wirt for President. Although Wirt only won the State of Vermont, ex-President John Quincy Adams was elected to the House of Representatives as a nominee of the Anti-Masonic Party.

There have been many notable historical figures that have been Freemasons, lists of which can be found in other publications e.g. "10,000 Famous Freemasons" by William R Denslow, 1957-60 and there is even an Internet Web page devoted to listing well known masons.

Much has been written in the past about Mozart's Masonic involvement and it is interesting to observe this against the background of the relationship between Freemasonry and Catholicism. Mozart was a Catholic and such was the esteem that the church had for him that at the tender age of 13 he was made a Knight of the Order of the Golden Spur by the Pope in Rome. Despite the Papal Bull of 1738 against Freemasonry, Mozart became a Mason in Vienna in 1784 obviously upsetting the church hierarchy. He immediately began composing for Freemasonry, the most notable works being K468 - The Fellow Crafts Journey (1785), K471 - The Masons' Joy (1785), K477 - Masonic Funeral Music (1785) and K483-4 - Lodge Opening and Closing Odes (1786).

Financially, Mozart was in dire straits and was known for availing himself of Masonic charity. In 1791 (the year of his death) he accepted a commission to write the music for The Magic Flute which is often regarded as his greatest musical accomplishment. This work caused a major controversy both in Masonic circles for giving away Masonic secrets to the public and in Catholic circles since it apparently celebrated the Masonic alternative to the Catholic Mass.

Mozart was very ill and with his financial difficulties he became melancholy and had premonitions of approaching death. He received a mysterious commission to write a Requiem Mass, the purpose of which was kept secret, and this only served to accentuate his fears to the point that he suspected that he was being slowly poisoned by his enemies. In fact he believed that it was his own funeral music that he was composing as the excerpt of a letter written by him in September 1791, reprinted in the Transactions of the Quatuor Coronati Lodge, 1974, shows.

Unfortunately, he did not complete this work before he died. There are two theories relating to his death: one was disease, the other that he had in fact been poisoned. Although he died in the Catholic faith, he did not receive the reserved sacrament probably because of his Masonic membership and at the same time having upset the Masons by making public certain Masonic secrets, there were no Brethren at his funeral. His body was sadly buried in an unmarked pauper's grave in Vienna.

Earlier in this chapter we mentioned the 1605 Gunpowder plot. We also mentioned that Lord Mounteagle's Brother-in-law, Francis Tresham was the likely candidate for leaking the plans. Mounteagle had another Brother-in-law, a Mr. Abingdon who owned a residence called Hindlip House (sometimes referred to as Hendlip Hall), near Worcester.

The following information comes from "Old England: A Pictorial Museum", edited by Charles Knight and originally published in 1847. After Fawkes' capture, a search was made for the other conspirators and a Humphrey Littleton who was condemned to death for harbouring two of the conspirators, told the sheriff of Worcester, in order to save his own life, that some of the Catholic priests mentioned in the royal proclamation, were hiding at Hindlip House.

Sir Henry Bromley was sent by the sheriff to make a search.

The building design was very intricate and full of extraordinary hiding places. After four days, two priests were found and after another four days, Henry Garnet was discovered. Garnet was the Superior of the Order of English Jesuits, an underground Catholic order, and had been knowledgeable about Guy Fawkes' intended mission. He was eventually tried, found guilty of conspiracy and executed.

During Bromley's' search of Hindlip House, he found eleven secret passages "*all of them having books, masoning stuff and popish trumpery in them.*" Knight concluded that "*this curious old mansion seems to have been built in great part for the express purpose of concealing distressed Catholics*". Perhaps the reference to "masoning stuff" indicated that it also concealed a Masonic Temple.

Hindlip House was pulled down about 1800 but according to Knight, writing in 1847, "*A manuscript now in the British Museum details the singular discoveries made in the course of the protracted search*". The author recently visited the British Museum, who told him that this document should still be in their possession but after an initial search they couldn't locate it easily as it was likely to be unindexed in a large archive but that a dedicated researcher may well uncover it. If it turns out that the "masoning stuff" is actually Lodge furniture from a previously unrecorded Masonic temple, dating from earlier than 1605, then not only would this be a major find in its own right, but it will cause much of Masonic history to be rewritten particularly those aspects that relate to the relationship between the Catholics and Freemasons.

In later years Hindlip Hall was a girl's school but was pulled down around 1800 with a new house built on the site in 1820. The house was designated as a potential home for the war cabinet in 1940 and is currently the headquarters of the West Mercia Police.

Hindlip House pulled down about 1800. Did it contain England's earliest known Lodge? (reprinted with permission from Portland House Publishers, New York)

9) Other Degrees and Orders

We have already discussed the ritual of the 1st degree in some depth. There are those Freemasons who derive much pleasure from the actual performance of the ritual. This appeals to those who might also join an amateur dramatic society.

After a Mason has been through all the Offices of the Lodge, he is not involved in the ritual anymore. If he yearns to take part or is still keen to pursue the elusive secrets, he can join another Lodge, start one of his own, or become involved in what are known as the "higher" degrees, side orders and other Masonic or quasi-Masonic bodies. By taking these higher degrees the Brother becomes part of the Masonic elite.

However, the majority of Masons are kept completely in the dark about these matters, believing that the three "craft" degrees are the be all and end all of Masonry. This is due to cleverly worded statements by the Grand Lodge of England that gives this impression since their only jurisdiction is over the three basic degrees and they probably do not want to lose any subscribing members. A section of the Constitutions (which are given to every new Freemason) entitled "Aims and Relationships of the Craft" has the following paragraphs:-

"The Grand Lodge is aware that there do exist Bodies, styling themselves Freemasons, which do not adhere to these principles and while that attitude exists the Grand Lodge of England refuses absolutely to have any relations with such Bodies, or to regard them as Freemasons."

"The Grand Lodge of England is a Sovereign and independent Body practising Freemasonry only within the three Degrees and only within the limits defined in its Constitution as "pure Antient Masonry". It does not recognise or admit the existence of any superior Masonic authority, however styled."

However, these paragraphs taken together mean that Grand Lodge does have relations with the very many Bodies that do share the same fundamental principles as themselves, provided that these Bodies recognise that Grand Lodge has sole jurisdiction over the 3 craft degrees. What Grand Lodge is actually saying is that although these other degrees are referred to as the "higher" degrees it does not mean that those bodies promoting them have any authority over Grand Lodge which specialises in the "lower" degrees.

For instance, the management and administration of the Royal Masonic Hospital, was conducted by subscribing Lodges belonging to the United Grand Lodge of England, the Supreme Grand Chapter of England, the Great Priory of England, the Supreme Council of the 33rd Degree of England and Wales *"as well as any other body of persons whose objects include the dissemination of Masonic knowledge."*

To gain access to the higher degrees, the Mason must have first completed the three basic degrees of Craft masonry.

What follows is a complete list of the additional Masonic orders. This information can be found quite readily in the public library. We have used as our main source a booklet by Fred Crowe, published in 1894 by George Kenning titled "The Master Masons Hand Book", which was probably also the source used by Walton Hannah in his 1952 exposure, "Darkness Visible".

Fred Crowe points out that although the Grand Lodge does not formally acknowledge the higher degrees, they are nevertheless held in the highest esteem and are eagerly sought after by the most eminent members of the Craft. At the time of Crowe's book (1894), the Grand Master, HRH the Prince of Wales, was also the Supreme Ruler of some of the additional degrees. It is also interesting to note that all the higher degrees were introduced after the formation of Grand Lodge in 1717.

Supreme Order of the Holy Royal Arch

Of the additional degrees, this is the only one actually attached to the Craft degrees and is the earliest known of the additional degrees having been introduced about 1737 to 1740. Originally part of the Third Degree, it was separated out and became loosely known as the 'Fourth Degree' although other commentators still regard it as the completion of the Third Degree.

This degree is concerned with the discovery of the "real" lost secrets as opposed to the "substituted" ones of the Craft degrees. Of those masons that go beyond the basic three degrees, most stop at this level. This degree is conferred in a Royal Arch Chapter and the ceremony of admission is called Exaltation. The ruling body of this Order is the Grand Chapter of which the Grand Scribe just happens to also be the Grand Secretary of Craft Masonry.

The use of a compound word to apparently denote the name of God in different languages and ancient cultures has given rise to much speculation that Freemasonry is a religion and furthermore that not only is God worshipped but also the devil.

Mark Masters Degree

This is also an ancient degree dating from the latter half of the 18th century. Originally there were two degrees, the Mark

Man and Mark Master. This degree is governed by the Grand Lodge of Mark Master Masons of England. Whereas the Grand Master of the United Grand Lodge of England is currently HRH The Duke of Kent, the Grand Master for the Mark Masons is HRH Prince Michael of Kent.

The ceremony of admission is known as "Advancement". One of the principles of Mark Masonry is that work produced by a mason should "bear upon it the mark of his private characteristics, and thus be recognised from all others". For this reason there is much interest in actual medieval stone masons marks.

A booklet dated 1938, "Masons Marks in Cyprus" privately circulated by J E Bowler, provides the locations and hand drawn illustrations of Masonic marks found on ancient sites, the earliest of which apparently dates from about 300 AD from the Great Forum in Salamis through to 13th and 14th century castles and churches. He refers to one mark that resembles a swastika and comments that the swastika first appeared on pottery in Cyprus as early as 2600 BC. Bowler was obviously trying to perpetuate the "time immemorial" myth of Freemasonry. A further point of interest concerning Cyprus is that Craft, Royal Arch and Mark Masonry was introduced to the island in 1888 by John Percy White, a Staff Sergeant in the Royal Engineers stationed at Limassol.

Royal Ark Mariner

Ark Mariner Lodges are "moored" to Mark Lodges. The ceremony of admission is called "Elevation" and Masons are permitted to join after they have achieved the degree of Mark Master. The ritual is concerned with the salvation of the human race through Noah and the Ark.

Grand Council of Royal and Select Masters

This council confers 4 degrees known as:- Most Excellent Master, Royal Master, Select Master and Super-Excellent Master, the system being collectively termed Cryptic Masonry as the ritual is concerned with the crypt beneath King Solomon's Temple in which Masonic secrets were apparently concealed.

The council was constituted and established in London on 29th July 1873 based on authority of the Grand Master of Royal, Select and Super-Excellent Masters of the State on New York, USA and the Grand Royal Arch Chapter also of New York on 6th July 1871.

To be eligible for these degrees, the Mason must have obtained both Mark and Royal Arch degrees.

Grand Council of the Allied Masonic Degrees

This ruling body was formed to take under its direction various Orders that recognised no central authority or acknowledged no common form of government. The five degrees controlled by this council at the time "The Master Masons Handbook" was published were those of St Lawrence the Martyr, the Knights of Constantinople, the Red Cross of Babylon, the Grand High Priest and the Grand Tyler of King Solomon.

Hannah states that there are a further 30 extinct degrees formally registered under the Allied Council. "The intention appears to be to keep them in cold storage to prevent their unauthorised revival".

Ancient and Accepted Scottish Rite

In 1974, the Deputy Grand Master of the Grand Lodge of

Scotland compiled a Register of Supreme Councils of the Ancient and Accepted Scottish Rite. In it he points out the Rite actually has no connection with Scotland.

It is believed that the Rite originated in France with the earliest recorded Chapter established in Paris in 1754 although Baigent, Leigh & Lincoln in "The Holy Blood and the Holy Grail", 1982, suggest that the Scottish Rite was devised by Charles Radclyffe who founded the first Masonic Lodge on the continent, in Paris, in 1725. On the other hand, Robinson ("Born in Blood") suggests that the Rite evolved out of Ramsey's Oration, a paper delivered at the Masonic Lodge of St Thomas in Paris in 1737, where Ramsey proposed a Masonic link between the returning Crusaders and Scotland where they apparently established the earliest Masonry in Britain. The Council for France established a Council for England and Wales in 1819 but the Head of the Order in England, the Duke of Sussex, allowed the warrant to lapse. The present Supreme Council was established in 1845 under the authority of the Supreme Council for the Northern Jurisdiction of the United States. The Order spread to Latin America and the West Indies where a Council was founded in Jamaica in 1770 and another body in Port Prince in 1796.

According to Crowe, the 33 degrees of this ritual are the most highly valued of all the additional degrees. The first three degrees are not worked by the "Supreme Council 33rd Degree for England and Wales" so that there is no clash with the three Craft degrees governed by the Grand Lodge of England.

The full list of the titles are as follows:-

1.   Entered Apprentice

2.   Fellow Craft

3.   Master Mason

4. Secret Master

5. Perfect Master

6. Intimate Secretary

7. Provost and Judge

8. Superintendent of Buildings

9. Elect of Nine

10. Elect of Fifteen

11. Sublime Elect

12. Grand Master Architect

13. Royal Arch (of Enoch)

14. Scotch Knights of Perfection

15. Knight of the Sword of the East

16. Prince of Jerusalem

17. Knight of the East and West

18. Knight of the Eagle and Pelican, and Sovereign Prince Rose Croix of Heredom

19. Grand Pontiff

20. Venerable Grand Master

21. Patriarch Noahite

22. Prince of Libanus

23. Chief of the Tabernacle

24. Prince of the Tabernacle

25. Knight of the Brazen Serpent

26. Prince of Mercy

27. Commander of the Temple

28. Knight of the Sun

29. Knight of St Andrew

30. Grand Elected Knight, K.H., Knight of the Black and White Eagle

31. Grand Inspector, Inquisitor, Commander

32. Sublime Prince of the Royal Secret

33. Sovereign Grand Inspector General

Any Master Mason is eligible for advancement to the degrees of the Ancient and Accepted Rite. He must have at least 12 months service as a Master Mason before he can be accepted to the 18th degree (Sovereign Prince Rose Croix). In England the degrees from 4 to 17 are not worked in full but are wrapped up in the ceremony of the 18th degree. Hannah points out that a 1950 Handbook listed 16,000 members of this degree that included 475 clergymen including 17 bishops.

Similarly, in England, the degrees from 19 to 29 are rolled into the ceremony of the 30th degree. The 30th degree is conferred by special selection of the Supreme Council. "No Prince Rose Croix (18th degree) is eligible to receive the 30th degree, unless he has been three years a member of the 18th degree".

The 31st and 32nd are also conferred by the Supreme Council by selection. The 1894 Handbook states that the number of members is strictly limited to a maximum of 90 31st degree members and 45 32nd members. By 1952, these numbers have increased to 400 31sts and 180 32nds.

From Crowe (1894) - "*The 33rd degree is conferred very sparingly by the Supreme Council, and only on Brethren of great mark and learning and high social position, hence its possession necessarily carries an unwritten patent of Masonic nobility with it. From its members, the Supreme Council is selected, the number being strictly limited to nine, and only one Supreme Council can exist in any one nation at the same time, unless under special circumstances, as in the United States of America*".

The United Religious and Military Orders of the Temple and of St John of Jerusalem, Palestine, Rhodes, and Malta

The degrees in this order are more commonly known as "Knight Templar" and "Knight of Malta". The earliest known reference to the Degree of a Masonic Knight Templar is from the records of St Andrews Chapter, Boston, dated 28th August 1769, when a William Davis was accepted and "made by receiving the four steps, that of Excellent, Super-Excellent, Royal Arch, and Knight Templar".

The qualification for membership is that candidates must be Royal Arch Masons.

Many authors, as mentioned earlier, have latched on to the existence of this degree as evidence of a Templar connection to the historical origins of Freemasonry.

Masonic & Military Orders of Knights of Rome and of the Red Cross of Constantine, Knights of the Holy Sepulchre, and Knights of St. John.

According to Crowe, there were about 100 Conclaves working these imitation chivalric degrees under the authority of the Grand Imperial Council. Whereas the degrees of the Red Cross of Rome and Constantine can be conferred upon Master Masons, the K.H.S and St. John are conferred in "Sanctuaries" and "Commanderies" upon Royal Arch Masons.

The Order of the Secret Monitor (or the Brotherhood of David and Jonathan)

The origin of this degree is American and by 1894 there were 21 Conclaves on the roll of the "Grand Council of the Order of the Secret Monitor in the United Kingdom of Great Britain and Ireland, and the Colonies and Dependencies of the British Crown". Its membership is drawn from Master Masons and according to Crowe contained some of the most eminent members of the Craft. Hannah describes part of the ritual which involves shooting arrows down the Lodge. Today, the Conclave numbers are up into the 300's.

The Societas Rosicruciana in Anglia (The Rosicrucian Society of Freemasons) - SRIA

This society was founded in 1866 by Dr William Wescott, a London coroner. The ritual is based on the rites and ceremonies of the medieval "Brethren of the Rosy Cross". Its members devote themselves to study and research into the "ancient mysteries" and the Kabbalah. Hannah describes the rituals as an "extraordinary hotchpotch of high sounding oriental mysticism and sham occultism". The nine degrees are conferred on Master Masons strictly by merit. Together with the Secret Monitor, the only title to them being Masonic is that their membership is recruited solely from the Craft.

It is interesting to note that a poem by Henry Adamson, "The Muses of Threnodie", 1638, includes the following lines: "*For we be Brethren of the Rosie Crosse; We have the Mason word, and second sight, Things for to come we can foretell aright....*".

Magus Incognito, author of "The Secret Doctrine of the Rosicrucians", 1949, writes that "*members of the Rosicrucian body are prominent in the councils of nearly all of the occult organisations and societies throughout the world - in fact, it is these persons who are the real leaven in the general mass, and who keep alive the "Sacred Flame of Truth" in them. Many Rosicrucians are also prominent in philosophic and scientific circles, and some of them are men quite prominent in the large affairs of the business and professional world, and in the ranks of statesmanship. Others are prominent in movements like the Labor movement and similar activities. Some are prominent in the councils of the various churches, and others are leaders in Masonry and similar secret societies*".

He continues "*The modern interest in the Rosicrucian Teachings dates back to the early part of the seventeenth century - about 1610, to be exact. At that time there were rumours of the existence of a society known as "The Brothers of the Rosy Cross", the officers and meeting places of which were not known to the public. The mysterious society was severely attacked by the ecclesiastical authorities and others, and was as vigorously defended by those who were interested in the general subject of occultism and the esoteric teachings. There were many spurious and counterfeit "orders" established during the following century and for that matter in nearly every century since, but none that have been able to show an undoubted connection with the original order. Some of the original teachings of the Rosicrucians have been incorporated in some of the higher degrees of Masonry, and have served a good purpose therein*".

Arkon Daraul in "Secret Societies", 1961, comments that Elias Ashmole was also instrumental in forming the spurious Rosicrucian Society of London and concocted its ritual based on a mixture of Masonry and the symbolism of the alchemists.

Concerning the above mentioned Orders, Crowe (1894) states "we may assure our Brother that we have given a complete list of all legitimate Degrees as now recognised, and that all others are spurious and worthless". Browsing through any current Provincial Masonic year book shows that these orders are still in existence today and the various degrees are still being worked.

As well as regalia costs, the members would have to pay joining fees. This income "opportunity" obviously opened the door for many unscrupulous entrepreneurs who created new Orders and conferred spurious degrees on the gullible for a price.

Arkon Daraul in "Secret Societies" tells the story of a man called Flaximus who was the Provincial Grand Master of the four United Masonic Lodges in Hamburg in 1781. Unknown to his fellow Masons, he was also running a Rosicrucian Order from whose members he obtained a good deal of money.

The Transactions of the Quatuor Coronati Lodge are also full of examples. In the 1978 issue, the story is told of Theodor Reuss (1855-1923) who is described as "*a Masonic charlatan who used Freemasonry for his own ends and made a living from the gullible*". The same article mentions John Yarker (1833-1913) from Manchester who "*conducted his various Masonic enterprises - of these the Antient and Primitive Rite of Memphis and Misraim was the most notorious - for his own financial benefit*".

Dr William Wynn Westcott, as well as the founder of SRIA, was also the Supreme Grand Secretary of the Swedenborgian Rite, another spurious masonic order.

The SRIA gave birth to the Hermetic Order of the Golden Dawn in 1888, which provides an interesting glimpse into the darker side of Freemasonry.

The Hermetic Order of the Golden Dawn

In 1888, Dr William Wescott, Supreme Magus of SRIA, and two other prominent SRIA members, Samuel Mathers and Dr William Woodman created a new order, known as the Golden Dawn. R.A. Gilbert in "The Golden Dawn Companion", 1986, points out that in 1799 the Rosetta Stone was discovered which enabled the Egyptian Book of the Dead to be deciphered in 1830. There was much interest in Occultism during this period and it is alleged that this trio, using manuscripts at the British Museum concocted a ritual that had an element of every branch of occultism including the Kabbalah, Alchemy, Astrology, Tarot, Astral Projection and the use of Talismans. They invented a mythical history and claimed that they had "rediscovered" long lost manuscripts that authorised them to work these rituals.

They borrowed the Masonic structure of offices and used oaths of obligation almost word for word with the Masonic Oaths. They also had Steps, Signs, Tokens and Words - again, very similar to Masonry. The criteria for membership included a belief in a Supreme Being, age over 21 years, a pledge to keep secret the existence of the Order, its name, its members and its passwords. The candidate was also required to pledge that once accepted they would persevere through the ceremony of their admission. Even their motto, "To know, to do and to be silent" was based on the Masonic motto of "Hear, see and be silent". However, they accepted women into their order, which is probably the only reason that the Golden Dawn was not officially recognised by the Grand Lodge.

It drew its members mainly from the SRIA and also the Theosophical Society (discussed later) and within six years there had been over 300 initiations with Temples set up in London, Weston-Super-Mare, Bradford, Edinburgh and as far afield as Paris, Chicago and New Zealand.

Some of the notable members recruited included W B Yates, the Irish poet and dramatist and winner of the Nobel Prize for Literature in 1923 and Constance Wilde, the wife of Oscar Wilde, who was himself a Mason. Sir Arthur Conan Doyle (another Mason) writing in "Early Psychic Experiences", 1924, recounts how an attempt was made to recruit him. A member of the Amen-Ra Temple, No. 6, Edinburgh, was William Peck who was the City Astronomer of Edinburgh as well as a prominent member of a Scottish Masonic Lodge.

Perhaps the most notorious initiate was Aleister Crowley, author of many books on Magic and the Occult and who Winston Churchill once referred to as "the most wickedest man in Britain". Crowley was also the Head of the Order of the Templars of the Orient (OTO) for England and is referred to in the Proceedings of the Quatuor Coronati Lodge as the "Most Holy, Most Illustrious, Most Illuminated and Most Puissant Baphomet, Rex Summus Sanctissimus 33, 90, 96 degrees, Past Grand Master of the United States of America, Grand Master of Ireland, Iona, etc."

Crowley described the OTO as a body of initiates in whose hands are concentrated the wisdom and knowledge of the following bodies:

1.   The Gnostic Catholic Church

2.   The Order of the Knights of the Holy Grail

3.   The Order of the Illuminati

4.   The Order of the Temple (Knights Templar)

5.   The Order of the Knights of St John

6.   The Order of the Knights of Malta

7.   The Order of the Knights of the Holy Sepulchre

8.   The Hidden Church of the Holy Grail

9.   The Rosicrucian Order

10.   The Holy Order of the Rose Croix of Heredom

11.   The Order of the Holy Royal Arch of Enoch

12.   The Antient and Primitive Rite of Masonry (33 degrees)

13.   The Rite of Memphis (97 degrees)

14.   The Rite of Mizraim (90 degrees)

15.   The Ancient and Accepted Scottish Rite of Masonry

16.   The Swedenborgian Rite of Masonry

17.   The Order of the Martinists

18.   The Order of the Sat Bhai

19.   The Hermetic Brotherhood of Light

20.   The Hermetic Order of the Golden Dawn

The Golden Dawn ceremonies were conducted at Mark

Masons' Hall in Great Queen Street but members were careful not to embarrass the Masonic authorities, being told that they *"must not enter Mark Masons' Hall by the front door, but go under archway and down passage, entering by a door on the right"*.

Short describes how the various senior members of the Golden Dawn became bitter enemies as they fought each other in a destructive power struggle.

One of the most prominent members of Craft Masonry apparently listed as a member of the Golden Dawn was Walter L Wilmshurst, author of the important Masonic book "The Meaning of Masonry", 1927. He was the "Past Provincial Grand Registrar for West Yorks, United Grand Lodge of England" and was a renowned historian and an acknowledged Masonic scholar. In the foreword to the 1980 reprint of Wilmshurst's book, Allan Boudreau, Ph.D., Curator and Librarian of the Grand Lodge of Free and Accepted Masons of the State of New York, states that *"The great value of this book is that it was written by one who sets an example for all Masters of Lodges"*.

If Wilmshurst was a member of the Golden Dawn, he laid himself open to expulsion from Grand Lodge since they admitted women into their order.

According to Grand Lodge's constitution, *"The membership of the Grand Lodge and individual Lodges shall be composed exclusively of men; and that each Grand Lodge shall have no Masonic intercourse of any kind with mixed Lodges or bodies which admit women to membership"*.

Rule 176 of the Constitutions states *"A person who has in any way been connected with any organisation which is quasi-Masonic, imitative of Masonry, or regarded by the Grand Lodge as irregular or as incompatible with the Craft, may not*

136

be initiated into the Craft except by leave of the Grand Master or the Provincial or District Grand Master, as the case may be".

"*A Brother who subsequent to his initiation has in any way been or is connected with any such organisation as above-mentioned shall be bound to disclaim and finally sever such connection, or on failure so to do when called upon to do so by any proper Masonic authority shall be liable to suspension or expulsion and shall not thereafter be entitled to a resumption of his Masonic privileges until he shall have petitioned the Grand Master, made due submission, and obtained grace.*"

Wilmshurst would have had to have had the Grand Masters permission to take part in this quasi-Masonic organisation or keep his membership of the Golden Dawn a dark secret.

According to Gilbert, the Golden Dawn was considered to be the cornerstone of all modern occultism. It effectively closed down in 1914 but the Hermes Temple No. 28, continued to operate in Bristol until 1960. The Golden Dawn still lives on today, as tapping into the Internet will reveal, and most specialist occult bookshops would contain many Golden Dawn magic books and Tarot cards.

The Headquarters of SRIA and Golden Dawn was based in Dr William Wescott's house in Camden Road, London NW. A collection of his papers concerning the relationship between the Rosicrucians, Freemasonry, the Kabalah, Astrology and Hermetic Philosophy can be found in another book by Gilbert entitled, "The Magical Mason".

The Independent Order of Mechanics

I used to drive by a Masonic looking building in Hackney, London as I made my way to join the main A12 road and stopped one day to take a photo. With its obvious Masonic symbols I was surprised not to find any mention of this organisation in any book about Freemasonry and could only find one Dutch website that had some information about it. Checking the Internet quite a few years later I found that there were a few more websites that give a little more information about this group including the group itself coming out into the open with its own official website at http://iuomwh.org.

The Independent Order of Mechanics started in the county of Lancaster in 1757 as a result of a schism between two Masonic Lodges and received its authority to operate from parliament. It was essential a type of mutual benefit society that also served ceremonial and friendship purposes. It admitted men and women although they were separated with the men meeting in Lodges and the women in Chapters.

The group's motto is "Friendship, Truth and Love". Members aim to practice and promote justice, philanthropy, charity and benevolence. They look after the welfare of their members and are active in their communities, particularly in healthcare and in education.

Its first six degrees (the Pink, Scarlet, Green, Blue, Red Knight and White Degrees) match almost word for word with the first three degrees of regular Freemasonry with further degrees almost identical to those of the York Rite (Mark Mason, Royal Arch and Knights Templar).

In the 1800's, it spread to the United States, Canada, Central-America, Holland and the Caribbean and appears to still be active today with a tradition of a strong African American membership. The World headquarters is in New York with http://alphadistrictgl.org being the website of the Alpha District Grand Lodge No.1, NY.

An out-of-copyright book entitled "A Concise History of the Independent United Order of Mechanics Friendly Society from 1847-1879" can be read on the Internet and the Resolutions of the Grand Council include such gems as people suffering from fits cannot be admitted as members whereas deaf and dumb candidates can be, that blindness did not qualify as a sickness for sick benefit purposes and that trespassing did not constitute immoral conduct. The resolutions show that the Order declined allowing the United Order of Free Gardeners to join their order only because the Mechanics did not allow people over the age of 40 to join.

In the UK, the Financial Services Authority (FSA) in 2007 cancelled its permission to allow the order to carry on regulated activities. Apparently it had not filed accounts for over six years and failed to satisfy the FSA that they had conducted their business soundly and prudently.

Independent Order of Mechanics

Ancient Order of Free Gardeners

I first came across mention of this group when studying the Resolutions of the Grand Council of Mechanics.

The origins of this Order are obscure but it seems to have started in Scotland in the middle 17th century with its principal aim of sharing of secret knowledge linked to the profession as well as being a benefit society. The early members of the first known Gardeners Lodge, Haddington established in 1676, were not gardeners by profession, but small landowners and farmers who practised gardening for pleasure. They attempted to fit their 'trade' into a wider story by drawing parallels with the original garden - Eden. Enthusiasts assembled a body of esoteric knowledge and ritual, borrowing freely from the example of Freemasonry and kept their rituals secret from non-members. Like Freemasonry, the order needed to find a link between the 'operative' gardeners and the 'speculative' gardeners who came from the aristocracy. The story goes that the order started by operative gardeners were joined by the aristocracy who owned large country mansions with magnificent formal gardens and wanted to learn more about horticultural advances that could be then be employed in their own estates. This sounds more logical than the Freemasons' explanation of why aristocrats joined Freemasonry.

The Lodge officers were the Master, two Wardens, Chaplain and Inside and Outside Tylers. There were three degrees: Apprentice, which was based on Adam, the First Gardener, in the Garden of Eden and where the Square and Compasses are used together with a Pruning Knife open at an angle of sixty degrees representing 'the simplest tool of gardening' allowing 'pruning the vices and propagating virtues by cuttings'. This degree also featured the Tree of Knowledge. The second degree is that of Journeyman, based on Noah, The Second

Gardener who makes the symbolic voyage towards the Garden of Eden and then on to Gethsemane which is a garden at the foot of the Mount of Olives in Jerusalem. This degree also features the ark, doves and a rainbow after the flood. Finally the third degree features King Solomon, the Master Gardener, and the pillars of the temple.

Principal emblem of the Free Gardeners

Each ceremony included an obligation, passwords, signs and a catechism. Aprons, collars and jewels of the Order show a similar symbolism to Freemasonry. The working tools of the order included the crossed spade and rake, watering cans, reel and measuring line, again similar to Freemasonry. A pineapple or a bunch of grapes were used to symbolise the skill of a gardener as only a master gardener had the skill to cultivate the fruit in 18th century Scotland.

Like the Freemasons, the Gardeners created their own a biblical mythology and creation story. Their regalia featured the letters PGHE which were the initials of the four rivers (Pishon, Euphrates, Gihon and Hiddekel) that flowed through the Garden of Eden. A further letter group, ANS, symbolises a word of recognition appropriate to each degree - Adam, Noah and Solomon.

One interesting fact is that the suppliers of the Gardeners' regalia were the established Masonic regalia suppliers – they simply adapted the existing Masonic aprons and sashes and other paraphernalia and now had a new marketplace into which they could sell their wares.

From Scotland it first spread to England and then to Ireland, Australia and the US. In 1911 there were 70-80 Lodges with a combined membership of 12,000. But Free Gardening was never able to compete successfully with Freemasonry for members and seems to have died out in the last quarter of the twentieth century. Some commentators believe it was because people didn't want to pay for sickness benefits as the National Health Service came into being whilst others think it was because of the rise of the non-ritual based horticultural societies that attracted those interested in gardening and the order petered out through the lack of new recruits. I think it was simply that the Freemasons were better recruiters and had the benefit of royal patronage.

Under the headline "Free Gardeners withers on the Vine", the Sydney Morning Herald (September 29, 2006) reports the closure of the Grand United Order of Free Gardeners because the corporate regulator said that it couldn't meet the new standards of compliance and governance. The main problem seemed to be the large amounts of money in the funeral fund and other investments as well as property that benefitted a smaller and smaller group of people as membership dwindled. This was known as the "Tontine effect" where the last man standing inherits the lot.

The regulator decided the members were not "fit and proper" persons to run the fund and wound it up. The remaining members were not too unhappy because they got to share out on a pro-rata basis the funds of $4.8 million (before tax) as well as the proceeds from selling their lodge building which was in the centre of Melbourne.

In 1997, Professor Jay Macpherson wrote a paper, "Masonic Landscape Design" published in the Transactions of Quatuor Coronati, which examined whether there was a connection between Freemasonry and gardening, particularly as the new English trend for large formal gardens in country estates was established about the same time as the Grand Lodge was formed in 1717. She concluded that there was no such connection and that this avenue of research was a dead end. Commentators on her paper pointed out that she had missed out referring to the Order of Free Gardeners and she replied that would read the forthcoming book "The Ancient Orders of Free Gardeners" which was being published by the Grand College of Rites, a "regular" Masonic body dedicated to preserving the history and rituals of defunct and inactive Masonic orders.

Robert Cooper, senior Scottish Freemason, Curator of the Grand Lodge of Scotland and author of many books on Freemasonry including "The Masonic Magician" co-authored with Philippa Faulks, published a small book in 2000 called "Introduction to the Origins and History of the Order of Free Gardeners". According to the speaker details for the 3rd International Conference on the History of Freemasonry to be held in Virginia in May 2011, Robert Cooper is currently a Free Gardener, so this raises the question as to whether the ancient order is still operating today.

With the focus today on preserving the environment and other green issues, it seems there is an attempt in the UK at reviving this order with the creation of the Modern Order of Free Gardeners. According to their website, the society is focussed on two things: "Our environment; how we work with it and preserve it and the history and philosophy of the original Ancient Order of Free Gardeners" (www.freegardeners.org.uk).

First established in 1887, The Gardeners Arms was once
owned by The Fraternity of Free Gardeners of East Lothian
(photo taken by "emdjt42" July 2012)

10) Religion

Although Freemasonry declares that it is not in itself a religion, many Masons are able to satisfy their religious needs through Freemasonry and to justify to themselves their lack of participation in a recognised religious organisation. At the same time Freemasonry does attract many men of the cloth to its proceedings who find that the solemn ceremonies are not incompatible with their particular faiths. However, Hannah's' "Darkness Visible", 1952, caused many Christian Masons much heart-searching as to the legitimacy of their dual allegiance, with many leaving the order. According to Martin Short, Hannah was ostracised by the Church of England for attacking Freemasonry and its strength among the bishops. He entered the Roman Catholic Church and died in exile in Canada.

The ceremonies are based around an acknowledgement of the Supreme Being - the Architect of the Universe. Other religious overtones come from biblical references, hymns, organ music and prayers led by the Chaplain. Meetings are held in Temples which are consecrated and have altars. When he dies, the good Mason ascends to those "blessed mansions" of Grand Lodge above. Freemasonry considers that a Mason belongs to the "universal religion" and therefore any discussion about a particular religion is banned in the Lodge.

The subject of religion has always been the subject of much debate. Trevor Stewart in the introduction to a reprint of "The Spirit of Masonry", 1775, by William Hutchinson (often referred to as "the father of Masonic symbolism") comments that one of the main charges that the Antients laid against the Moderns was "that their ritual had been deliberately de-

Christianised". Stewart believed that Hutchinson's book was intended by Grand Lodge to refute that accusation for it purports to demonstrate that profound religious themes form integral parts of Freemasonry, particularly in the Third degree. The public attitude of the day can be summed up by quoting from Hutchinson - "*In this age, when everything serious is received with laughter, everything religious treated with contempt, and whatever is moral, spurned from the doors of the polite; no wonder if my intentions to prove this society a religious as well as a civil institution, is ridiculed and despised*'.

W.L. Wilmshurst, respected Masonic authority and probable Golden Dawn member argues that Freemasonry is basically another expression of the Gospels. He complains "*By a tacit and quite unwarranted convention the members of the Craft avoid mention in their Lodges of the Christian Master and confine their scriptural readings and references almost exclusively to the Old Testament, the motive being no doubt due to a desire to observe the injunction as to refraining from religious discussion and to prevent offence on the part of Brethren who may not be of the Christian faith*'.

He argues that the New Testament is essential to the Masons' instruction, it being full of passages in Masonic terminology. He believes that the three Masonic degrees map directly onto the three ceremonial degrees of admission to the early Church where "*Their first degree was that of a rebirth and purification of the heart; their second related to the illumination of the intelligence; and their third to a total death unto sin and a new birth unto righteousness, in which the candidate died with Christ on the cross, as with us he is made to imitate the death of Hiram, and was raised to that higher order of life which is Mastership*'.

A similar theme is argued by Bishop Charles Leadbeater in

"The Hidden Life in Freemasonry", 1926, who equates the 3 degrees of Freemasonry to positions in the Church, respectively, Subdeacon, Deacon and Priest. He equates the Worshipful Master with Bishop.

In an ARS review of the French book, "La Franc-Maconnerie Templiere et Occultisre" (Templar and Occult Freemasonry) by Rene Le Forestier, 1970, funded by the French National Research Scientific Centre, it is stated that the author claims that the 1738 constitutions prove that the origins of the Craft was definitely of a Christian character and that "the religion on which all men agree" alludes exclusively to this religion and that Jews or members of any other non-Christian religion were excluded from membership. Religious tolerance was valid only for members of the different Christian sects.

In contrast to this, it is said (Cecil Roth, "A History of the Jews in England", 1964) that the coat of arms of English Freemasonry was designed by Rabbi Judah Leao who exhibited a model of the Temple of Solomon at Court in 1675 and also that Jews held high office in English Lodges as early as 1723.

Catholics, though, were forbidden from joining Freemasonry by various papal decrees, the earliest reference being Pope Clement XII in 1738. His bull which condemned Masonic beliefs and observances as being pagan and unlawful, threatened excommunication for any Catholics who joined. Robinson ("Born in Blood") provides a full English translation of the original Latin text of "Humanum Genus", the strongest papal condemnation of Freemasonry by Pope Leo XIII in 1884.

One criticism of Freemasonry made by Pope Leo is the complaint that "*they deliberate and preserve the habits and customs of secret societies. Nay, there are in them many secrets which are by law carefully concealed not only from the profane, but also from the many associated* [i.e. masons]".

Leo XIII's main thesis was that Freemasonry was associated with the Kingdom of Satan. Stephen Knight in "The Brotherhood" used this reference to arrive at the conclusion that Freemasons were devil worshippers. Robinson interprets the text as follows:- "*What the pope actually said was that the Salvation Army, the Baptist church, the Buddhists, and the Mormons - in fact, every member of the human race who was not a Roman Catholic - was part of the 'kingdom of Satan'.*" If Robinson's explanation is correct, why did the Pope only single out the Masonic Sect, "*in order to illustrate more and more this wicked force and stop the spread of this contagious disease*"?

The answer lies in the fact that Freemasonry accepted members from all faiths. The "Antient Charges" confirm "Let a man's religion or mode of worship be what it may, he is not excluded from the order, provided he believe in the glorious architect of heaven and earth". As part of the initiation ritual the candidate is informed prior to taking the Oath that there is nothing in the obligation that is "incompatible with your civil, moral or religious duties" which is designed to remove any final hesitation on the part of the candidate. The Popes view though, was "by opening their gates to persons of every creed they [masons] promote, in fact, the great modern error of religious indifference and of the parity of all worships, the best way to annihilate every religion, especially the Catholic".

By the 1800's, the international influence of Grand Lodge had grown significantly ("*that society of men spread all over and solidly established, which they call Free-Masons*") and it was not only affecting recruitment into the Catholic faith whose duty was to "*continue to increase all over the world by new additions*" but the Church was also losing too many existing members to Freemasonry.

Arkon Daraul in "Secret Societies", 1961, comments that Freemasons and Catholics hold almost precisely similar ideas about each other, namely that each consider that the other *"constitute a dangerous secret society which is dedicated to the overwhelming of the world"*.

The justification for many Catholics joining Masonry apart from the apparent compatibility with their religious beliefs was the Masonic commitment to the practice of Charity. Pope Leo's real intention in his decree was, on the one hand, to halt the exodus of Catholics who were persuaded to join Freemasonry, but on the other and perhaps more importantly, to promote its own competition to Freemasonry, the Society of St. Vincent de Paul, which was more *"fit for the exercise of Christian charity and the relief of human miseries"*.

Society of St. Vincent de Paul

As with many large organisations, this society was founded by a small group of committed individuals who shared a common cause. The 1958 publication of "The Manual", the rule book of the Society, explains that the group was founded in Paris in 1833 by a 20 year old named Frederic Ozanam who set up a "Conference of Charity" to enable Catholic students away from home to meet regularly and exercise a form of charity. They had no thoughts of founding a large organisation; rather they sought to bring some assistance to the homes of a few poor persons.

The papal hierarchy started to promote this society and despite objections from the founders, the society expanded to a point where a superior management authority was set up, known as the Council-General, to oversee the affairs of the society and promote recruitment. A rule book was published establishing the authority of the Council-General and its subordinate bodies, the Metropolitan Central Councils and the Superior Councils.

Within a few years, branches were set up in Rome (1842), England (1844), Belgium, Scotland and Ireland (1845), Germany, Holland, Greece, Turkey, Mexico and USA (1846), Switzerland and Canada (1847) and Austria and Spain (1850).

Pope Gregory XVI issued a document in 1845 establishing further rules and regulations concerning the organisational structure. It also recommended the Society of St. Vincent de Paul to the wider Catholic community and by 1850 the society had grown to 2500 branches embracing some 50,000 members. Its annual income was almost 4 million francs.

As the society continued its rapid growth, there were concerns about its political muscle. Between 1860 and 1870, both the French and Spanish governments took measures against the society which they regarded as a possible centre of opposition. With laws passed in France banning the Council-General, it continued its recruitment activities in North and South America.

By 1913 there were 8000 branches with 133,000 members and an income of 15 million francs. After the 1st World War, the society was able to penetrate places where it was hitherto unknown, and groups were established in China, Japan, the Malayan Archipelago, Indo-China, Burma, India, Ceylon, Madagascar and East Africa.

In 1933 there were centenary celebrations which consecrated this world-wide expansion with 33 countries represented and in each country, government officials associated themselves with the commemorative functions. By 1953, there were over 20,000 branches with an active membership of a quarter of a million.

The Manual informs us that the society which is neither a religious Congregation nor a Brotherhood, is essentially Lay in character and membership, but with the management in the hands of the Church authorities. For a long time the society took refuge in obscurity and although through its growth it became known to the public, its members are still instructed to "remain in the shadows".

The society is a purely male organisation although a ladies section was started in Bologna in 1856 which was entirely distinct from the male society. In fact, the society is strictly forbidden from occupying itself with charitable works relating to solely women, this being the province of the women's society.

Like Freemasonry, new branches wishing to set up have to get dispensation from the Council-General. Members wishing to travel and visit other branches have to apply through the Secretary of the Council-General who will make the appropriate arrangements.

The organisation of each branch includes an elected President and appointed officers such as Treasurer and Secretary. At the weekly meetings, the President deals with the admission of candidates whose names had been sanctioned at the preceding meeting ("*Each member should be careful to introduce into the Society only persons likely to edify their fellow members*"). The Secretary's task is to keep a register of the names, occupations and addresses of the members with their dates of admission and the names of the proposers.

Other similarities with Freemasons are that members are banned from discussing politics at their meetings, are encouraged to recruit new members and to constantly study their Rule book which is "*our fundamental charter, and it is our duty to preserve it with the greatest respect*". All branches are kept constantly in touch through the monthly communications of Council-General known as the "Bulletin". Today, this international Catholic organisation boasts more than one million members world-wide with active branches in 115 separate countries.

Coming back to Church of Rome's view of Freemasonry as argued in 1925 by Rev Joseph I. Malloy in "May Catholics be Masons?", after about 250 years, on the 19th July 1974, a Declaration was made which finally permitted Roman Catholics to join Freemasonry. This document was the first time that the Holy See admitted the existence of a Freemasonry which was not antagonistic to the Church of Rome. However, Benimeli, author of an article "Catholics and Masonry" in a Spanish magazine "New Life", 25th January 1975, complains about the hypocritical attitude displayed in the last sentence of the Declaration (Canon 2335) which still absolutely prohibits Clerics, those bound by monastic vows, and members of secular institutes from joining any type of Masonic association.

In 1981, the position reverted and excommunication for Catholic Masons applied once again. Martin Short's view is that this "Masonic love affair" coincided exactly with the period 1974-81, during which time the infamous P2 Masons had infiltrated the Vatican.

In January 1994, the Grand Master's wife, the Duchess of Kent, was the first member of the Royal Family to convert from Church of England to Roman Catholic and it was hoped that this might have a positive effect upon the relationship between Freemasonry and Catholicism. However, freemasons Knight and Lomas have probably done much to harm this relationship. In their 1996 book, "The Hiram Key", they accuse the early Catholics of taking over the organisational movement built up around Jesus and inventing myths and religious beliefs to support and advance their own political ends. They quote Pope Leo X as commenting "it has served us well, this myth of Christ".

They allege that the beginning of the Christian Church had nothing to do with Jesus himself but was the invention of Paul. Paul, who was not a Pharisee rabbi as others had claimed but a simple adventurer from an obscure background, was the henchman of the High Priest who hunted down rebellious Jews.

When he was disappointed with his chances of advancement, he split with the High Priest and invented his own religious cult. He gave his movement the Greek name "Christians" (a translation of the Hebrew word for messiah) and called Jesus, a man he never knew personally, "Christ". This "hijacker" of Jesus started to build a following around himself and "stole" the teachings of Jesus' community for his own teachings.

Paul was closely involved with the Romans and they saw the possibility of Christianity as advancing their own political aims. "*The Roman Empire had been a hugely successful political force, but despite its ruthless approach to holding power its might could not last forever. It began to crumble as a cultural force but it found that the control of the minds of people was far more effective than just controlling their bodies. Christianity gave Rome the mechanism to establish unparalleled political might based on unsophisticated masses who would be offered a better life after death if they did the Church's bidding*".

The early Roman Church set about destroying everything that did not meet its required dogma and invented new texts that supported their objectives. If the plebeians had to have their superstitions, the Romans eventually reasoned, why not have one that was state controlled? Constantine "*had a complex web of superstition woven to wrap up the minds of the masses to keep them in their place. His vision for the common people was to use them to produce goods and wealth in peacetime and provide soldiery in time of war; their reward for their sad, ignorant little lives was the promise of their own personal resurrection and a wonderful afterlife*".

The inventors of Christianity altered the legend of a local saint and removed all evidence about a mortal they wanted to portray as a god. By this method, the Bishops of Rome gained unchallengeable power and incontestable authority over those who "had faith".

Knight and Lomas conclude that the survival of the organisational and theological structure off the Roman Catholic Church has always been dependant on the suppression of the truth and that the "*bejewelled Vatican and its offspring are the true pagans and heretics*".

The Mormons

According to Deborah Laake in "Secret Ceremonies, A Mormon Woman's Intimate Diary of Marriage and Beyond", 1993, Joseph Smith, founder of the Mormon church, was an enthusiastic Mason.

Perhaps this Masonic interest influenced him when in 1827 he claimed that he had found the lost secrets of an ancient people, descendants of the biblical Hebrews. According to Smith, a heavenly messenger directed him to some gold plates buried in some nearby hills that were inscribed in a hieroglyphic language. "*By the gift and power of God*" he translated the plates and produced the "Book of Mormon" after which the plates were apparently returned to the angel and never seen again.

Smith stated that he had received divine authority to appoint himself to the office of priesthood and start the Mormon church in 1830. Regarded as a prophet, he attracted a small band of followers and by 1837 was sending missionaries overseas (mainly to England and Scandinavia) to recruit converts and persuade them to emigrate to the United States and join his sect. The most successful recruiter was one Wilford Woodruff who managed to convert 599 out of 600 farmers at a mass meeting in Herefordshire.

Also in 1837, to fund his activities, Smith started his own bank and began to print bank-notes with only minimal capital to back them up. When the authorities withdrew his license to operate a bank, he simply renamed it "The Kirtland Safety Society Anti-Banking Company". It folded and Smith was fined $1000 (Daily Mail 6/4/95).

Today, Mormonism is a major world religion with more than 8 million members, 4 million of which are in the United States. In recent years, Mormonism has grown rapidly in the Third World. In Mexico, 600,000 people were converted to Mormons between 1975 and 1992 and in South Korea there were more than 100,000 by 1990. A steady influx of new members is generated by a rotating force of about 45,000 young men and women who devote 2 years of their life as missionaries.

Mormons pay a compulsory tithe (tenth of their income) in order to support numerous church activities. During August 1995, the Mormon church started buying up farmland in England. They purchased 4600 acres in Cambridgeshire adding to the 300 acre dairy farm it already owned in the Midlands. It then bought another 5000 acres in Norfolk and Suffolk making its land ownership to about 10,000 acres. This put it into the top ten of Britain's land owners following the Crown, the Duchy of Lancaster and Railtrack.

Smith's Masonic influence is still felt (literally) by members today. Deborah Laake explains that Mormon women have to wear a special type of undergarment. These garments have the Masonic symbols of the square and compasses sewn into the left and right breast areas to remind the wearers that they should "*deal squarely with their fellow men*".

Liberal Catholic Church / Theosophical Society / Co-Masonry

As there is no formal recorded history of the origins of Freemasonry, there is nothing to stop an individual developing his own theories and these can become quite incredible when they get mixed up with religion. As an example we are going to examine the case of Bishop Charles Leadbeater.

Leadbeater was of the 33rd degree in a branch of Freemasonry known as Co-Masonry. Co-Masonry accepts women and is therefore not recognised by Grand Lodge but in all other respects it complies with the same principles and conducts the same ceremonies. In the foreword to his book referred to earlier, Dr Annie Besant (journalist and mistress of George Bernard Shaw), points out that although the book is primarily aimed at members of the Co-Masonic order, she also recommends it to members of the "masculine Craft". Elsewhere in the book she is referred to as "the Very Illustrious Bro. Annie Besant, First Lieutenant Sovereign Grand Commander of the Co-Masonic Order".

She introduced Co-Masonry to England in 1902 and afterwards to India. Part of English Co-Masonry, was a section called "The Fellowship of Crotona" which was a secret order of witches and it was through this vehicle that Gerald Gardner revived witchcraft in England in the mid-twentieth century.

Leadbeater was a curate in the Church of England and then

became a bishop in a new church known as the Liberal Catholic Church. He held a belief that Jesus Christ, the original World Teacher, was also the "Head of all True Freemasons throughout the World" (HOATF). He tracks various personalities throughout the centuries supposedly incarnations of HOATF. These personalities include Albanus (St Albans - died 303 AD), in 411 - Proclus, 1214 - Roger Bacon, 1375 - Christian Rosenkreutz (supposedly the founder of the Rosicrucians), 1425 - Hunyadi Janos, 1500 - Robertus, 1561 - Francis Bacon, 1660 - Jozef Rakoczi, in the 18th century - Comte de St Germain and then a Baron Hompesch. Leadbeater claims he met HIM personally in Rome in 1901 but doesn't tell us his name. Leadbeater proposed that the HOATF was spiritually connected with whoever holds the rank of Sovereign Grand Inspector General of 33rd degree of Co-Masonry which was probably Leadbeater himself at that time.

As a point of interest, the Comte de St Germain, referred to above, was well known for practising Masonic and Rosicrucian rituals in Germany and France during the eighteenth century. According to Manly Hall writing in "The Freemasonry of the Ancient Egyptians", the Comte attempted a "*restoration of certain secret, metaphysical systems not practised in human society for 1500 years*". One of his notable disciples was Anton Mesmer - often regarded as the father of hypnosis.

Not too much is known about the Comte's origin although he was believed to have been a Portuguese Jew, born in 1710 and died about 1784. He knew most of the European languages, was a musical composer and a capable violinist and his accomplishments as a chemist were considerable. He is purported to have had the secret for removing flaws from diamonds and transmuting metals. In 1743, he was arrested in London for being a Jacobite spy.

Rachel Storm in "In Search of Heaven on Earth", 1991, tells about Madame Helena Blavatsky, a Russian princess born in 1831, who deserted her ageing husband and travelled the world earning her keep as a mediums' assistant and bareback rider in a circus. During her travels she was apparently initiated into esoteric Buddhism in Tibet and following this, she founded the Theosophical Society in 1875 "*to promote a knowledge of Theosophy, which is the cornerstone of all major religions, that embodies the accumulated wisdom of the ages, handed down from one generation to next by enlightened seers of whom every civilisation and culture bears ample record*". By starting her own society, she was able to achieve the "enlightened seer" status amongst her followers.

Lewis Wolpert, writing in the Literary Review, April 1993, reviewing Peter Washington's book "Madame Blavatsky's Baboon", tells us that the Theosophists believed in a Hidden Brotherhood that oversees the affairs of the planet, revealing themselves, rarely, to a chosen few who may, if they follow instructions, join them. As a point of interest, inside the Universal Shrine at the Theosophical Society's international headquarters at Adyar, Madras, India, pride of place is given to the Masonic symbols of the square and compasses.

Amongst their fans were notable talents such as Yeats (also a member of Golden Dawn), Aldous Huxley and Katherine Mansfield. Wolpert concludes that the Theosophists and their followers were searching for something mystical which their normal life failed to give them and that many of the same dissatisfactions with materialism and science are present in our society today. Mde Blavatsky's publication, Lucifer, carried the first public statement of the Hermetic Order of the Golden Dawn.

Co-Masons, Annie Besant and Charles Leadbeater were also leading figures in the Theosophical Society. Mrs Besant became the Society's president in 1907 following Mde Blavatsky's death in 1891. One area of interest for the Theosophists was the legend of the Holy Grail and in 1908, Annie Besant assisted fellow Theosophist, Herbert Whyte, to found a children's group, The International Order of the Round Table. In the 1930's, the Round Table became an independent movement. Both Maria Montessori and Rudolf Steiner, founders of their respective school movements, were also active Theosophists.

Mary Lutyens in her book "The Years of Fulfilment", 1983, tells us that the Theosophists at that time believed that Christ (the World Teacher) was about to reappear in human form again. About 1909, Leadbeater picked a young Indian boy out of a crowd on a beach and claimed that he had discovered the "vehicle" for the next incarnation of the World Teacher. The boy's father was a Theosophist and Mrs Besant persuaded him to let her become the boy's legal guardian. Leadbeater appointed himself the boy's teacher and set about indoctrinating him in the philosophy of the Theosophical Society.

Two years later (January 1911) Besant formed an organisation called the "Order of the Star in the East" which had the object of preparing the way for the coming of the World Teacher. The boy was made Head of the Order. His name was Krishnamurti and he was only 15 years old.

Krishna was sent to England to be educated and it was hoped that he would eventually go to Oxford or Cambridge. However, he failed his matriculation, his main interests being golf and tinkering with his motor bike.

After further involvement with Theosophical members, he became interested in the movement and started to take part voluntarily in their meetings. He was soon giving lectures on the subject of Theosophy and became regarded as something of a guru.

By 1927 he was beginning to have doubts about the Theosophists view that he was the "vehicle" or chosen one to be the incarnation of the World Teacher. At the same time he rejected Leadbeater's attempts to get him to accept Co-Masonry and be the incarnation of the HOATF.

He developed the belief that the only genuine way to the "Truth" was through an individual's own path of research and not through any organised religion, sect or society. His mission became one of setting men "absolutely and unconditionally free".

In 1929, at a mass meeting, to the horror of over 3000 followers and believers he disbanded the Order. Later that year he resigned from the Theosophical Society.

He went on to become a world renowned speaker arguing against organised beliefs. He would always preface a talk with the declaration that did not represent or belong to any sect or society *"for organised belief is a great impediment: these societies and religions are fundamentally based on vested interests and exploitation"*. He not only maintained that ceremonies were unnecessary for spiritual growth but that such societies actually prevented the individual from growing.

Aldous Huxley became a close friend and often quoted Krishna as saying *"There is life in men, not in a society. All organised beliefs are based on separation, though they may preach Brotherhood"*.

In 1972 Krishna was saying that knowledge of the truth could not be achieved through an "intellectual mythology". "Creating a mystery out of nothing would be a most blackguardly thing to do because that would be exploiting people and ruthless -

that's a dirty trick". Similarly, Thomas Paine in criticising organised religions in the 18th century said, "truth never envelops itself in mystery; and the mystery in which it is at any time enveloped is the work of its antagonist, and never of itself" (Thomas Paine, "The Age of Reason", 1795).

In 1980, Krishna was still travelling the world meeting international figures and preaching that the answer to many of the world's problems was through individuals own discovery of the "truth" which would lead to true harmony, compassion and Brotherhood. "*Men cannot come to it through any organisation, through any creed, through any dogma, priest or ritual, not through any philosophical knowledge or psychological technique*". Krishnamurti died in 1986.

Rachel Storm comments that at its height, the Theosophical Society had millions of members throughout the world. Today, it still has branches in some sixty countries with a membership in excess of 33,000.

11) A School Lesson

Masons are taught that Freemasonry is "a peculiar system of morality, veiled in allegory and illustrated by symbols". Moral principles are taught through analogy and stories. The following story again illustrates the principle of how a group started with one purpose in mind can be hijacked or moulded into something else entirely.

In 1996 I met with Andrew Hogg, Evening Standard reporter and co-author along with fellow reporter, Peter Hounam, of a book called "Secret Cult" published in 1984. The book tells how one man created an organisation founded on a certain belief that soon expanded to the point where the organisation itself took on a different personality with a different set of objectives and eventually became a full blown religious cult.

Andrew MacLaren was born in Glasgow in 1883. As a teenager he developed a fanatical love of Mozart to whom he referred to as his own musical god. He was also interested in economics and politics and joined the Labour party. About 1935, whilst the Labour MP for Burslem, he founded an economics study group called the School of Economic Science (SES), the main aim of which was to promote his belief in the institution of land value taxation. George Bernard Shaw once said of him, "If I were Prime Minister, I would make Mr MacLaren, Minister of Land".

His son Leon (Leonardo da Vinci MacLaren), a London barrister, also supported this economic principle and as old age crept up on Andrew MacLaren, he relinquished control of the group to his son. As a point of interest, Leon stood for the Labour party in Epping but lost to Winston Churchill.

In 1947, the year that Leon took over control of the SES, it became a formally constituted trust, so that subscribers to the funds of the School could enter into deeds of covenant.

Leon radically altered the identity of the School and its main objective was re-defined "to promote the study of natural laws governing the relation between man in society and to promote the study of law, customs and practices by which communities are governed".

During the 1950's, the SES adopted the teachings of two 20th century mystics, George Gurdjieff and Pyotr Ouspensky. They claimed to possess an ancient knowledge which had been handed down through the ages in a series of esoteric schools particularly a school called the Universal Brotherhood. Gurdjieff was also an accomplished hypnotist. According to Rachel Storm, "*the secret knowledge that Gurdjieff had acquired and that captured the imagination of thousands was, put simply, that man is a machine*". In a manner similar to Krishnamurti, Ouspensky, towards the end of his life, renounced his beliefs and shocked his disciples when he declared "*there is no system*" and that they had to look elsewhere for the truth. Today, though, the SES still regards itself as the latest in a long line of esoteric schools which has safeguarded this secret knowledge.

In 1961, MacLaren organised the first world assembly of the Maharishi Mahesh Yogi (the Beatles' guru) at London's Royal Albert Hall and introduced Transcendental Meditation to the West. It was also in 1961, that MacLaren gave up his work as a barrister and devoted all his energies to the SES. He introduced rigid rules and demanded greater commitment from the followers who were in the main, a highly educated intelligent group of people from the upper strata of British society.

This strengthened commitment brought the SES financial gains. The SES was granted tax relief as an educational charity. The membership fees were kept low but the donations, bequests, endowments and covenants ensured that the coffers were never empty.

Millions of pounds have been raised with much of this invested in property including the headquarters, which was housed in a prestigious building in Queens Gate, Kensington. In the 1970's, a country mansion in Oxfordshire was purchased where MacLaren now lives, as well as a mansion on the edge of Hampstead Heath in London, two further adjoining properties in Queens Gate and premises in Sheffield and Manchester.

In 1976, the SES was gifted Necker Island in the Caribbean by a wealthy British member, which was later sold to Richard Branson of Virgin Records for $300,000, about £180,000.

As the fortunes of the SES prospered, its control over its members grew even tighter. Its beliefs centred on a Supreme Being, referred to as the Absolute. It claimed that the further a person was from the Absolute, as in the case of a new recruit, the more rules they needed to bring them closer to it. They state that personality prevents realisation of the Absolute and therefore it needs to be suppressed and eventually eliminated.

Those of an individualistic turn of mind often do not last the initial course. They either leave of their own volition or the SES tutor makes it apparent that their presence is not welcomed. Right from day one, the movement is carefully selecting those who seem likely to meekly obey the cults' rules although *"some spirit is desired - it is easier to chip away at an abrasive surface than a totally smooth one"*.

The technique used to suppress personality, was applied in a teaching environment and was known as "taking the Measure".

This technique is handled extremely skilfully by the SES trainers for unless a convert has been properly primed, they are likely to be frightened off by these methods. By leading them gently towards it, the result is usually, a colossal tightening of the hold the school has on their life.

With the technique firmly established, the SES member embarks on a voyage of self-discovery where all maps and compass-points are supplied by the cult.

These developments were particularly worrying to Leon's father, Andrew MacLaren, founder of the SES. It was reported that he attempted to gain entry to one of the meetings being held at Church House, headquarters of the Church of England at Westminster but his way was barred by a group of SES members guarding the door of the room. He died in 1975 aged 91.

Leon MacLaren has exported the SES to other parts of the world with great success. In only 30 years it has become an international movement with possibly hundreds of thousands members. In Holland, for instance, where the branch started in 1962, within 20 years it had enrolled over 22,000 members recruiting mainly from the well-educated and well-groomed Dutch professional and executive class.

The SES London headquarters became the central clearing house for start-up funds, lecture material and advertising copy. Care was taken to make sure that SES followers in whatever foreign branch received the same systematic programme of indoctrination.

SES has members in influential positions in many walks of life. In this way it differs markedly from other religious cults, many of which do not seem to appeal to what marketing experts would denote as A-B category customers. Hounam and Hogg name many well known personalities from the world of politics, the judiciary, business, the Church and Trade Unionism as members of the SES.

As with Freemasonry, it is the secrecy that surrounds the SES that causes so much interest in its operations. Secrecy permeates every aspect of the SES operation with the code of silence impressed on members from the very first term of their involvement. Members are trained not to act spontaneously, emotionally or without authorisation. The SES is a disciplined force in which the lower ranks are not encouraged to ask questions or query decisions.

The only material the SES has ever produced about itself for public consumption has been pamphlets aimed at recruiting new members and letters to newspapers objecting to criticism.

The SES has attracted criticism from around the world. In Holland there is a strong anti-SES movement consisting mainly of ex- members who have gone public about its recruitment methods and secrecy. In a Dutch radio programme, an SES leader appeared in order to counter criticism. To avoid blatantly lying, which would have shattered many members faith as they were devoted to "The Truth", he used "double-speak" so instead of "religion" he said "philosophical system" and for "secrecy and evasion" he referred to the "radiant light of conscious silence".

A Maltese newspaper stated, "*A few very unfortunate members remained attached to the group because they had become fascinated through the application of suggestion methods, reinforced by regular trance-like exercises and other auto-suggestive practices. They remain captive within a circle of select clubmanship bestowing upon themselves a sense of respectability and intellectuality. These poor misguided individuals, albeit adult, give one the impression that they are living in a state of delusion and that they are completely unaware of being taken for a ride."*

The New Zealand press also criticised the group for its secrecy. The reply was *"we don't seek publicity and neither do individuals within the organisation. We are not a secret society. Other groups like the Public Service also had rules about not speaking publicly on its private affairs"*.

In 1980, Hounam and Hogg interviewed many ex-members. In most cases strict anonymity had to be guaranteed before people were willing to talk. Many people found it difficult to come to terms with what they considered to be their earlier gullibility.

Former members have claimed that the School practises subtle brain-washing techniques to ensure absolute obedience. They are forbidden from discussing the schools activities with non-members and if they leave the movement they become pariahs to those that remain.

Bishop Hook, quoted by Hounam and Hogg, said when questioned on his association with the SES said *"The impression I have been given is that, although they appear to be a syncretistic body very much based on Platonism, their chief offence is the same as the Masons, namely their secretiveness"*. It would seem that there are many other similarities between Freemasonry and the SES.

Hounam and Hogg conclude that the SES, which started as a harmless economic study group has become a more powerful and widespread cult than either the Moonies or Scientologists. Despite the furore created by their book in the 80's which caused many parents to remove their children from the SES schools, one of their schools is still advertised in the Independent Schools Yearbook attracting parents by the low tuition fees. Also, their posters luring potential recruits to SES evening classes in philosophy and economics are still to be found scattered around the London Underground system.

Leon MacLaren died in 1994. The current leader of the SES is Donald Lambie.

SES Poster on London Underground

12) Recruitment

Freemasonry has grown to its present size through a process of continuous recruitment. The only threat to its continuation would be if the levels of recruitment fell dramatically so that there was a shortage of new candidates being processed, which is the reason why individual Lodges close down. Without candidates there can be no ritual and without the ritual there is no purpose to the Lodge.

Most major changes in policy can be viewed in the context of response to falling recruitment levels. An example of this can be seen in Grand Lodges' reaction to Stephen Knight's "The Brotherhood" of 1985. This book concentrated quite a lot on the bloody penalties contained in the Masonic Oath that awaited a Mason should he break the code of secrecy. This attracted a fair amount of negative publicity which in turn affected recruitment levels.

One of the "Antient Charges and Regulations" read to the Master Elect prior to his Installation into the Chair is "*You admit that it is not in the power of any Man or Body of Men to make innovation in the Body of Masonry*". However, in December 1986, Grand Lodge changed this by adding effectively, "except Grand Lodge". This then enabled Grand Lodge to change the ritual of the Initiation ceremony so that the reference to the bloody punishments could be moved to a later part of the proceedings, after the part where the candidate swears the Oath of secrecy. Although they are now referred to as "the symbolic penalties at one time included in the Oath of a Freemason" they still have the same psychological impact on the "newly made" mason.

Knight and Lomas point to another time in the early 1900's where "*changes have been made to the ritual due to pressure on Grand Lodge from sources outside of Masonry*".

One reliable source of recruitment was from a Masons own family, particularly his son who was accorded a special Masonic status and was known as a "Lewis". However, Robinson in "Born in Blood" points out "*the concentration on individual morality and group charity has not halted the erosion of recruitment, as young men more frequently decline to follow their fathers and grandfathers into the Craft*".

Robinson also tells us that "*the social status of Freemasonry in Britain has been assured in years past by the patronage of the Royal family, but that too, may be changing. Prince Charles is the first British male heir to the throne to reject Masonry in almost 200 years*". This fact has reduced the impact of the "Charge after Initiation" which boasts of Freemasonry "*that in every age, Monarchs themselves have been promoters of the Art*".

Events around 1993 regarding Prince Charles' marital situation in relation to the Oath sworn by a third degree candidate to "*maintain a Master Masons honour, and most strictly respect the chastity of those nearest and dearest to him in the persons of his wife, sister and child", would have proved awkward if he had held the position of Grand Master. Even the Archbishop of York (Daily Mail 25/1/93) has recently questioned the role of the Royal Family's future as head of the Church of England because of Prince Charles' behaviour. Possibly in response to this attack, Charles is reported (Sunday Times 26/6/94) as planning to break the royal link with the Church of England. He argues that he should be a figurehead for all religions in Britain and that he should not be prevented from marrying a Roman Catholic.*

Another problem for recruitment today is the attack by certain organisations under the banner of promoting an open and free society. For instance, certain Local Authorities now require potential employees to declare their allegiance to any secret societies. This same movement was behind an unsuccessful attempt to introduce a ten minute bill into the House of Commons on June 28th, 1988, intended to curtail the acceptance of Freemasons into the Metropolitan Police. The proposer commented "*it is justifiably claimed that Freemasons are responsible for many laudable charitable activities. I unreservedly accept and applaud that but if only Freemasonry were to transform itself and shed its secrecy, exclusivity and oath of allegiance, I should have no objection to police officers becoming members*". In the debate it was also pointed out that over 50% of Chief Constables and 50% of the Police Federation were members.

A parliamentary debate in 1989 on Policing in London again referred to this issue with phrases such as "*we need more stringent measures to stamp out Freemasonry in the force. We must discourage young officers from joining the Freemasons and encourage older officers who are Freemasons to leave*". Recently, Kensington and Chelsea council drafted a code of conduct making it compulsory for all employees to declare any membership of a Masonic Lodge (Daily Express, 13/5/95).

The 1993 Blackpool conference of the Police Federation, debated whether officers who were Freemasons, should declare their membership publicly. The Conference Chairman (under instructions from above?) failed in his prior attempt to have this item completely removed from the agenda. During the conference, as reported in the Daily Telegraph, 21st May 1993, a Masonic police officer complained that "*those who sought to distort and misrepresent the Masonic message, ignored the large amounts of money raised for charity and the fact that Masonry stood firmly for virtue and good citizenship*" - a typical response to any criticism. A woman PC responded "*that until such time as the Masonic Order comes out of the closet, it has no place in the police service*". In the event, the attempt to get police officers to publicly declare their membership of Freemasonry only failed by 391 votes to 492. It will only be a matter of time before this gap is finally closed.

When the Chairman of the John Lewis Group declared his 25 year Masonic membership in his company's staff newsletter, his disclosure caused a storm of protest among the staff with many demanding his resignation.

In July 1996, the Southend Borough Council voted by 14 to 5 on a resolution to force councillors to declare their membership of Freemasonry. A number of Masonic councillors stormed out of the meeting in protest. The mayor stated that he recognised the work that masons did for charity but the move was based purely on the desire to remove any secrecy from local politics. The council also passed a resolution requiring Council employees who were masons to be named on a register maintained by the town clerk and open to inspection by members of the council.

Occasionally, Freemasonry strikes back. Concerning an inquiry into Freemasonry within the London Borough of Hackney, the Grand Master wrote in April 1995 "*many of you know about the Hackney inquiry, but it is remarkable that while we quickly implemented three recommendations to improve Freemasonry's relationship with local authorities, we still have no news of six recommendations on how the Borough might improve its administration*".

Today's world is also witnessing a change amongst those organisations that have for so long been "men only". Masons totally reject the idea of women becoming involved especially as it is forbidden in the ancient charges. They ridicule those women that have formed their own Masonic Lodges even though their husbands are often senior Masons within Grand Lodge.

Women have recently not only been successful in breaking the 600 year closed shop within the Church by winning ordination rights but members of the ruling General Synod have decided to rewrite prayers and services to make them more acceptable to feminists (Daily Mail 13/7/94). Even the "Who's Who" indicates the loosening of the old school tie in favour of increased representation by women (Sunday Times 31/1/93). Another example, is that in 1993, the West Kent Golf Club, which like many others up and down the country, maintain a men-only rule in their club bar, became the first golf club to have its' drinks license renewal application refused by magistrates and a Crown Court judge on the grounds that they discriminated against women. Freemasonry is simply another challenge.

A factor of the current economic situation is the extremely high level of unemployment and a growing sense of insecurity amongst those who previously believed that they had a job for life. This is affecting all levels of staff from company directors downwards. The sector of the population from which Freemasons are traditionally drawn, are perhaps less able to cope with this changing world having only known one particular lifestyle. Taking time off for Freemasonry and the costs associated with it, are now not such a high priority and Masons in influential positions in business are also much less able these days to help "Brethren in distress" with offers of employment.

We have already seen in the chapter concerning the Initiation, the advice giving to Masons in 1981 by the Grand

Master designed to encourage recruitment. In December 1993, a newsletter from Grand Lodge again reminded the Masons of this advice on how to solicit for new members. An indication of the recruitment crisis was contained in a newsletter from the Assistant Grand Master, October 1993, circulated to all Brethren which comments that the falling membership, particularly in London, was a cause for concern. "*If there is one thing that is obvious, it is that the future well-being of London Lodges depends on a commitment by all Brethren both to attract new members and then to retain their interest. It necessarily follows that if we are to attract suitable candidates into our Lodges, we must be prepared to talk openly about Freemasonry. Let me make it clear, however, that I am not advocating disclosure of the 'secrets' in our ceremonies. Brethren, let our solicitation remain proper, but let us be more active and less reserved about it*". This same problem was again referred to in the December 1994 newsletter.

This is a world-wide problem for Freemasonry as recent postings to the Internet newsgroups demonstrate:-

"*The Grand Lodge of Ohio has had a declining membership since about 1971 at a rate of 3 to 3.5% per year. This is expected to accelerate over the next 12 years as the ageing membership, brought into Masonry in the late 40's and 50's will be too old to continue active support. Ohio hit its peak in membership in 1959. We are experiencing approximately a net loss of 5,000 members per year.*"

"*Of our 395 members, 282 are aged 60 years or more. That's almost 3/4. In the 10 year age groups, the largest is 70-79 with 128 members. What's even more alarming, we have more members who are over 80 than we do who are in the 21-40 groups. If this trend continues, our lodge will certainly be in trouble*".

A small article in the London Evening Standard (9/9/94) gives an indication of the panic setting in - "*Freemasons are launching an advertising campaign aimed at policemen and civil servants in magazines and newspapers. The adverts are for the promotion of an official history of Freemasonry, but they accept it could encourage applications to join them and say they would welcome such requests*". One advert appeared in the Christmas Gift Guide section of the Daily Mail on Saturday, October 15, 1994. Buried amongst mail order offers for fleecy joint warmers, shopping trolleys, back ache cushions, silk lingerie and a confidential telephone service for wives and relatives of prisoners on the run, this official advertisement from Freemasons Hall prominently displays the Masonic Square & Compasses symbol with the slogan "FREEMASONRY - Its No Secret"! On offer is the "History of English Freemasonry" book and tape set and at only £44.95 it is proclaimed to be "an ideal gift".

In today's world of equal opportunities and political correctness, the future for Freemasonry looks very bleak. Frederick Glen points out "*an organisation that fails to perform a useful function, no longer fulfils the basic reason for its existence*". Even Freemasons are beginning to question its validity -"*our biggest criticism of Freemasonry is its sheer pointlessness. It does not know where it came from, no one seems to know what it is trying to achieve, and increasingly it seems improbable that it can have much of a future in a world that demands a clarity of purpose and benefit*" (Knight and Lomas).

13) Mind Control?

My first degree is in Experimental Psychology (BSc) and I took two Masters courses in Occupational Behaviour and Health Psychology. I have also attended an Introduction to Stage Hypnosis course run personally by Paul McKenna's (world renowned hypnotist) first mentor. So I feel reasonably qualified to explore this particular subject. It is my contention that the Masonic rituals, in particular the initiation ceremony contain elements mind control or conditioning that binds the new Mason into the organisation.

In "Introduction to Modern Behaviourism" (1970), Rachlin describes Behaviourism as a branch of psychology, the object of which is to discover laws describing the behaviour of organisms. Learning, in particular, is a process by which relatively permanent changes in behaviour occur as a result of practice or experience.

One form of learning of which Pavlov (1849-1936) was a proponent, is Classical Conditioning in which a person learns to associate a response with a stimulus (event) to which it was not originally related. Pavlov's most famous experiments were with dogs where they were conditioned to salivate to the sound of a bell. Pavlov also conducted a lot of research into the physiological basis of hypnosis.

In 1898, Thorndike laid the groundwork for a paradigm known as Instrumental or Operant Conditioning. His basic principle was that one effect of successful conditioning was to increase the probability that a particular behaviour will occur again in similar circumstances.

B.F.Skinner's (1904-1990) methods of Instrumental Conditioning have produced the simplest, most powerful and most accurate of learning methods and he is particularly well known for developing apparatus known as the Skinner Box.

The very heart of the conditioning process is the establishment of a correlation between some aspect of behaviour and reinforcement and psychologists concern themselves with predicting whether a given event will reinforce a given behaviour. Reinforcers can be either positive or negative, in other words, reward or punishment.

Skinner discovered that the frequency of the reinforcement had a profound effect on behaviour and that there was a relationship between the method of reinforcement and the length of time it took for a particular behaviour to stop occurring (extinction) after the reinforcement was withdrawn. In certain circumstances, the response can be made nearly permanent by reinforcing it at scheduled intervals.

Of particular interest to this analysis into Freemasonry, is the finding that the promise of reward or the threat of punishment can have the same effect on an individual as an actual reward or punishment.

Sociologists also have something to offer in trying to understand the processes at work in Freemasonry. "Sociology" by Macionis, 1989, provides a useful overview of this subject. A lot of research has been carried out into the dynamics of groups, how members of a group conform to cultural patterns and how the pressures to conform can be quite considerable.

The pressures to conform are of two kinds; the fear of exclusion and the rewards of security and support which follow acceptance (Frederick Glen, "The Social Psychology of Organizations", 1975).

The demand for conformity is not limited to ones immediate social circle and interaction with unfamiliar people in group settings can generate considerable pressure towards conformity. Just how powerful these forces can be was revealed in a classic experiment conducted by Solomon Asch in 1952 where individuals chose obviously wrong answers concerning lengths of lines because the rest of the group did as well. This showed how people are prepared to compromise their own judgement in the interests of group conformity.

One of Asch's students, Milgram, also conducted what is regarded as a classic experiment when he was attempting to understand the principles at work during World War II, where millions of innocent people were slaughtered on command. His experimental design involved people being instructed to give apparently harmful electric shocks to others. The overall implications of Milgram's work is that people are surprisingly likely to follow the direction of "legitimate" authority figures and are also strongly influenced by others in their group even when those others are just "ordinary" people.

Another significant researcher was Irving Janis who was intrigued by the idea that people can be led to engage in behaviour that violates common sense. His findings suggest that even the powerful, such as United States presidents, are not immune to group pressure towards conformity. Often such groups develop a distinctive language and that members of the group may come to see others with more open minds as the "opposition". The result, Janis concluded, was "groupthink", meaning a reduced capacity for critical reflection.

One aspect of group dynamics is the concept of ingroups and outgroups. An ingroup is a social group with which people identify and toward which they feel a sense of loyalty. Ingroups and outgroups are created by the process of believing that "we" have valued characteristics that "they" do not have. Research has shown that the members of ingroups hold unrealistically positive views of themselves and unfairly negative views of various outgroups.

Frederick Glen explains that the techniques employed to produce such effects have reached a considerable degree of sophistication, not only in legalised situations, such as war, but in a wide range of contrived or manipulated group rivalries in politics, religion, sport, etc.

Guy Arnold ("Brain Wash", 1992) points out that "*most people are committed to a religion, a political party, a way of life or a set of dogmas to which they cling and for each of which they claim superiority to rival beliefs. Many people will adhere to these personal beliefs throughout their lives and any questioning of them is much more likely to be treated as an assault than as a reasoned enquiry*". "*Whenever an investigation touches upon an area of particular concern to an individual - religion, for example - he or she will 'switch off', unwilling to have a favourite dogma or shibboleth questioned. It is this very unwillingness to question a belief that is the greatest aid to indoctrination in all its forms, since most people find it hard to recant and admit that a lifelong adherence to a belief has been a mistake. In a majority of cases a person who comes across something contrary to his own perceived opinions will either ignore it or change the rules rather than admit that, perhaps, his own opinion is grounded in false assumptions*".

Social groupings range from informal networks which designate a web of social ties that links people together through other people, to more formal type of structure such as the "normative" organisation where people join in order to pursue some goal they believe to be morally worthwhile receiving personal satisfaction and social prestige for their efforts. Arnold comments, "*parallel to the need of people to belong to an interest group is the tendency of big organisations to level people down to a common denominator where it is harder to be an individual rather than just a member of the group.*"

Organisations tend to become bureaucratic with rules and regulations guiding the tasks of the members with a hierarchy established so that each person is supervised by someone higher up in the organisation and may also supervise others in lower positions. Bureaucratic organisations recruit carefully selected personnel and thus limit the variable and unpredictable effects of personal tastes and opinions.

Max Weber (1864-1920) noted that once fully established, bureaucracy is among the social structures which are the hardest to destroy. "Bureaucratic Inertia" is the tendency of bureaucratic organisations to persist over time and often means that such organisations will devise a justification for persisting long after they have outlived their usefulness.

Robert Michels (1876-1936) pointed out the tendency of bureaucracy to spawn "oligarchy" which is the rule of the many by the few. He was concerned that ambitious officials can use their access to information, opportunity to influence others and numerous other advantages to promote their personal interests. Since abuse of organisational power may not be readily evident to the public at large, Michels feared that the expansion of formal organisations might undermine society's control over its elected leaders.

One type of social grouping that offers useful insights in Freemasonry is that of the Cult of which there is no universally accepted definition by sociologists and psychologists. Cults are formed around a body of beliefs, not necessarily religious, which are expressed in customs, rites and ceremonies. Cults do not ordinarily stress doctrinal issues or theological argument and refinement as much as they emphasise the individual's experience of a more personal and intense relationship with the divine. Mysticism is frequently a strong element and they stress the attainment of individual power and excellence via the pursuit of cult practices. (Grolier 1993)

Some cults have a flexible, functional leadership and others have mentors who control and orchestrate cult events. Cult activity, which is often esoteric, generates a sense of belonging to something profound and of being a "somebody". The modern cult may be reviewed as a cultural island that gives adherents an identity and a sense of meaning in a world that has somehow failed to provide them with these things.

Ian Haworth is a leading campaigner in trying to warn society about the dangers of cults and is a consultant to the police and the Church. He is the General Secretary of the Cult Information Centre (CIC) which is concerned about the use of deceptive and manipulative methods used by cults to recruit and indoctrinate unsuspecting members of society.

In an article in the Daily Mail (April 21st 1993) after the Waco incident, he described how he, as a "hard-headed businessman", was recruited into a cult. Using very powerful psychological techniques, he was persuaded in a period of just 4 days to give up his job, hand them all his money and to dedicate his life to their organisation. Fortunately for him, an incident happened two weeks later which broke the spell, but it took nearly a year for the "wounds" to heal entirely.

In his article, he points out that research shows that those who join cults are of average to above-average intelligence. Nobody willingly joins a cult, they are recruited. Standard sales techniques are used to get the prospect to the first meeting where the mind control begins.

The power of the group is used to dominate the individual - a use of peer pressure that continues throughout the life with the cult. It all happens in the most determinedly cheerful way but any disbelief is described as "negativity".

In return for the benefits of membership, the member is asked for just a little commitment at a time, "it seems churlish to refuse", he comments. Ian Haworth describes how these cults are able, during a weekend, to effectively eliminate the personality and identity of the recruit by using mind control techniques. These include isolation from rational references, guilt, fear and the removal of privacy. The two basic principles of psychological coercion used by cults are a) that sudden changes in environment lead to heightened suggestibility and to drastic changes in attitudes and belief, and b) by making a person behave the way they want then they can make that person believe the way they want.

The CIC state that the methods used by cults include:-

HYPNOSIS - Inducing a state of high suggestibility.

PEER GROUP PRESSURE - Suppressing doubt and resistance to new ideas by exploiting the need to belong.

CONFUSING DOCTRINE - Encouraging blind acceptance or rejection of logic through complex lectures on an incomprehensible doctrine.

METACOMMUNICATION - Implanting subliminal messages by stressing certain key words or phrases.

UNCOMPROMISING RULES - Inducing regression and disorientation by soliciting agreement to seemingly simple rules.

DRESS CODES - Removing individuality by demanding conformity to the group dress code.

FINGER POINTING - Creating a false sense of righteousness by pointing to the shortcomings of the outside world.

FLAUNTING HIERARCHY - Promoting acceptance of cult authority by promising advancement, power and salvation.

FEAR - Maintaining loyalty and obedience to the group by threatening soul, life or limb for negative deeds.

All of the above processes feature in Masonic rituals.

Haworth points out how the new cultist regularly attends meetings and sees a whole roomful of identical clones all unquestioning, all dogmatic, all reacting to the same stimuli and able to spout meaningless dogma in the cheerful conviction that black can be white if the cult leader says so.

Another common factor is that all cults see themselves as an elite - separate from, and above, the rest of society. Outside reality is kept well away. Eventually, the world is simply divided into the Good, the members, and Evil - everybody else. All criticism is equated with persecution. It is an assumption of every cult that the rest of the world is either evil, or "negative", or out to destroy them. In the world of Freemasonry, outsiders are referred to as the "profane", which means blasphemous and offensive. In the end, the cultist loses all ability to doubt. There are no longer any problems or mysteries, for everything has an answer.

According to the CIC, cults want people who are: intelligent, idealistic, well educated, economically advantaged and intellectually or spiritually curious. The cults are after their free, lifetime commitment as a recruiter and fund-raiser (as in Freemasonry?).

Hounam and Hogg in "Secret Cult", 1984, quote R.K. Heller, author of "De-programming for Do-it-yourselfers: A cure for the common Cult" who examines how cults, which seldom use physical coercion, hold in their sway thousands of men and women. *"The Cult is a sect of people wherein victims hypnotise each other, inadvertently and unconsciously, with disguised methods yielding the apparent belief that no control is involved'*.

The person is told things that they do not understand and they are not given enough time to rationally analyse what is being said to them. He adds that by arousing guilt and fear, a person can be made more suggestible, and the suggestibility will increase the more the emotions are played on.

He believes that the reason why cult members feel such compulsion to continue with their membership is because the context where hypnosis takes place, be it a meeting, a meditation session or whatever, no provision is made for the hypnotic suggestion to be removed. In the same way that subjects do not believe that they have been hypnotised, a cultist does not believe he is being controlled.

The definition of hypnosis is another area where there is a lot of debate. The most up-to-date references define hypnosis as *"a state or condition in which the subject becomes highly responsive to suggestion. The hypnotised individual seems to follow instructions in an uncritical, automatic fashion. These effects may be extended posthypnotically into the individual's subsequent waking activity. It is as if suggestions given during hypnosis come to define the individual's perception of the real world'* (Grolier 1993).

"Hypnosis may be induced by a variety of monotonous practices and rituals that are found in many mystical, philosophical and religious systems. A profound trance is

characterised by a forgetting of trance events and by an ability to respond automatically to posthypnotic suggestions" (Encarta 1994).

A little known area of hypnosis research is that of the "hypnodrama" which has usually been used in a therapeutic setting ("Group Hypnotherapy and Hypnodrama", Ira Greenberg, 1977). Mass hypnosis is apparently relatively easy to establish in a group and a hypnodrama is where the "players" interact with each other on a "stage". The physical contact, movement and interaction of the players create very strong bonds. The players are "warmed up" by the use of familiar signs, gestures, words and actions. Other important preliminaries are bodily contact, embrace, handshakes, walking together and confusion (as in Freemasonry). J.L. Moreno, the developer of this technique, comments on the thought processes of a central player, "*he sees himself acting, he hears himself speaking, but his activities and thoughts, his feelings and perceptions do not come from him, they come, strangely enough, from the other participants*". Hypnodrama also has an effect on the audience ("Psychodrama and Audience Attitude Change", Greenberg).

In the hypnodrama, the players become profoundly affected by the scenes they are acting out and in this state of heightened suggestibility; an individual's "inner world reality" can be dramatically altered. In the "hypnodrama" of the 3rd degree ceremony, where the candidate acts out a death and resurrection scene, we can perhaps gain some insight into what "making" a Mason actually means.

Some insights into Stage Hypnosis can be gleaned from the experiences of Nobel prize winner for physics, Richard Feynman, recounted in "Surely you're joking Mr Feynman", 1985, where although he didn't believe he was being controlled by the hypnotist, nevertheless, he complied with the instructions. When attempting to fight the suggestions by taking an alternative course of action, "an annoying feeling came over me - I felt so uncomfortable that I couldn't continue". He analysed the experience and concluded "all the time, you're saying to yourself, 'I could do that but I won't' - which is just another way of saying that you can't".

Robert Temple in his book "Open to Suggestion - The Uses and Abuses of Hypnosis", 1989, quotes the common belief about hypnosis; that one cannot be made to commit any act against their moral principles under the influence of hypnosis. He boldly states that this view is not true and provides various examples to illustrate this fact. He devotes a large section to the subject of "waking hypnosis". He states categorically that *"you can be in a hypnotic trance and still be wide awake. This may come as a surprise to most people, but it is true beyond a doubt. It is generally thought amongst the public that trances can only occur when someone appears to be sleeping or nearly sleeping. But this is not necessary"*.

He continues *"An interesting report was published in a hypnosis journal in 1965 by Dr Hallack McCord. In it he recounted his experiments of hypnotising people while they were wide awake and engaged in normal daily tasks including those typical of those encountered in office and factory situations"*.

The first full scientific report on waking hypnosis was published in 1923 by Wesley Wells who recounted that he had hypnotised hundreds of people in the waking state. Banyai and Hilgard writing in 1976 state *"there is a large body of evidence, outside the experimental and therapeutic settings, suggesting the possibility of inducing hypnotic-like altered states of consciousness by manoeuvres designed to increase tension, alertness and physical activity rather than by relaxation and sleepiness"*.

Ludwig and Lyle in 1964 state that "*subjects in the waking trance state were less critical of commands and suggestions and seemed primed to respond automatically to the words of the investigators*". The subjects were instructed to pace the floor, spin around the room and then stand completely rigid. While the subjects were doing these things, they were bombarded with commands of various kinds and made to fear that they were in danger. In this situation, the researchers found that the subjects manifested a high degree of suggestibility. Temple concludes that "*at last hypnosis researchers in the lab were duplicating the kind of thing one could find in practice in countless tribal cultures around the world. It was producing what had been known to mankind for thousands of years in connection with religious and healing rituals*".

Neuro-linguistic Programming (NLP) is a method of inducing a hypnotic trance in someone through the use of a particular style of language which could be buried in ordinary conversation. Rachel Storm comments that NLP, a technique which aims to access the programming function within individuals at a deep level, bypassing normal forms of communication, is used widely by the Army as well as by the business world for sales and management training and by leaders of today's "New Age" cults. In the foreword to Grinder and Bandlers' book, "TRANCE-formations: Neuro- Linguistic Programming and the Structure of Hypnosis", 1981, it is stated that "*Trance experiences have existed in different forms for centuries, usually surrounded by a mystique of something magical and unexplainable. What is unique about this book is that it turns the "magic" of hypnosis into specific understandable procedures that can be used not only in doing "hypnosis" but also in everyday communication*". This book also provides an interesting insight into the use of a handshake as a method of hypnotic induction.

It was mentioned above that Freemasonry probably borrowed and adapted the rituals of earlier secret societies. Georg Luck in his book, "Arcana Mundi", 1985, suggests that it is the hypnotic induction process itself that is "the secret", unknown to those involved that was handed down through the ages via these types of societies. "*Hypnotism was probably practised in antiquity. The technique of inducing (in the absence of drugs) a trancelike state in a person and thus rendering that person more susceptible to external suggestions and directions is probably very old and may have been handed down as a secret in certain sanctuaries in Egypt and Greece*".

Knight and Lomas comment "*it has long been established by cultural anthropologists that information is effectively passed on to successive generations by tribal ritual without the exponents necessarily having any idea of what they are transmitting. In fact it is widely agreed that the very best way of transmitting ideas without distortion is via people that do not understand what they are saying*".

Arkon Daraul in "Secret Societies", 1961, states that "*the study of 'brainwashing' and conditioning the mind within the past decade has helped to lay bare the essence of the mysteries, and has answered the riddles which surrounded them*".

"*Initiation ceremonies of secret cults of the mystery type invariably involve tests, sometimes most severe ones. The effect of certain experiences was a carefully worked programme of mind training. This process produces a state in which the mind is pliant enough to have certain ideas implanted: ideas which resist a good deal of counter-influence. This is the secret of the mysteries, this and nothing else. Suffice it to say that the most primitive secret societies known to man, carry out ceremonies, rituals and processes which are not to be distinguished from those employed by modern brain washers*".

"The custom of having degrees of initiation has in many cases been taken advantage of, to inculcate different views of the world - or of the object of the Society - into the minds of the initiates as they proceed from one stage to another. This process is one of the marks of the less primitive, more sophisticated society which practises initiation, preparation and secrecy."

Often *"the 'conditioning' technique is employed to make the new member submissive to certain rules and to certain elders or chiefs"*. Also *"in the secret initiations belonging to primitive and highly developed religions alike, the initiate may believe that he has experienced contact with a divine power which may henceforth guide his steps."*

Daraul could almost be commenting exclusively on Freemasonry (which is conspicuous by its absence in his review of secret societies around the world) when he analyses the mechanisms that are used to achieve the desired effects which include:

- The desire to participate in the ritual, and expectancy of something happening

- Noise

- Threats or frightening happenings, generally staged and not genuine perils

- Symbolic death and resurrection

- The use of special signs and signals and 'key phrases' which will help to awaken the conditioning (training) for special or general purposes at different times

"Secret societies use this training system to take advantage of the human propensity for obedience to repeated or inculcated

189

stimuli. Professor Hutton Webster ("Primitive Secret Societies", 1908) was one who showed with remarkable clarity that the supernatural beliefs of the initiators were far less important than the fact that they were working effectively upon the minds of the initiated, and not necessarily for altruistic motives. The work of those who have pointed out the function of the mysteries as mind-training and conditioning has, of course, evoked no answer from those who still think that the rituals are mere symbolic representations of knowledge or of facts."

Through the Internet, one can connect to F.A.C.T Net (Fight Against Coercive Tactics Network, a non-profit computer bulletin board and electronic library) and download a document that helps define whether a group is a dangerous and destructive cult. This explains that a cult is authoritarian in its power structure. The leadership is regarded as a supreme authority. Power is delegated to a few subordinates for the purpose of seeing that members adhere to the leaderships' wishes. There is no appeal outside of this system to greater systems of justice. The cult has basically only two purposes, recruiting new members and fund-raising. The cults may claim to make social contributions but in actuality, these remain mere claims or gestures. The cult claims to offer the only viable system for change that will solve the world's ills. While claiming this, the cult then surreptitiously uses systems of psychological coercion on its members to inhibit their ability to examine the actual validity of the claims of the leaderships and the cult.

Guy Arnold attempts to differentiate between those forms of brain washing that can be seen as the necessary teaching processes upon which any society depends, and the more insidious and dangerous forms of brain washing designed to manipulate people into behaviour patterns that are solely for the benefit of the ruling elite. "*Brain washing, however defined, is essentially the deliberate manipulation of people's minds. What does and does not constitute brain washing cannot be defined with any precision. At one end of the scale come those techniques with which everyone is familiar, learning by rote, repetition, saluting, rituals, and learning deference to authority".*

"Those in the business of manipulation use varying human emotions as the basis for their persuasion techniques playing upon anger, fear, hope, guilt, pride and ambition. Loyalty is a key weapon in reinforcing the system and is a potent brainwashing tool. Loyalty always outlasts proof that it is no longer deserved."

Why should this information be the basis of a secret handed down through the centuries? From the earliest days of civilisation, individuals or groups of individuals have attempted to control the masses for their own ends. The knowledge of how to do this had to be kept secret from the wider society in general and specific enemies of the group in particular otherwise not only would the techniques employed be ineffective but also the groups' activities would be exposed. Also, this knowledge in the wrong hands could cause untold havoc.

Much of this knowledge was published in "Psychologie des Foules" (The Crowd: A Study of the Popular Mind) by Gustave Le Bon, 1896. This book is regarded as a classic on which the whole science of crowd psychology was founded. Brian Inglis in "TRANCE - A Natural History of Altered States of Mind", 1989, explains that Le Bon presented a theory to account for the way in which people in groups behaved in ways in which, as individuals, few of them would have been likely to behave. In such circumstances, intellectual control was weakened whereas instincts, passions and feelings are strengthened.

Robert Temple states with some certainty that one of the most important sources of Hitler's ideas as set out in "Mein Kampf" was Le Bon's "The Crowd", which "*is so simply written that a 10 year old child could quite happily read it*". Temple warns us that "*the plain simple fact is that Hitler's misuse of Le Bon's ideas was the greatest antisocial abuse of hypnosis so far in history. And what is more, it could be repeated*".

I pointed out earlier that the initiation ceremony uses devices such as sensory deprivation, discomfort, embarrassment, loss of balance, etc., to create a situation where the candidate is easily manipulated to accept that he took the Masonic Oath of his own free will and to condition him to accept the authority of the senior officers, contribute to the charity fund when requested and to keep the details of the ceremonies secret for all time.

Robert Lomas in "Turning the Hiram Key", 2005, also identifies these aspects of the ritual but his viewpoint is that these techniques are designed to heighten the candidates' awareness so that he enjoys the experience more.

Martin Faulks says "*According to Lomas (who is a solid state physicist) the ancient rituals contain trigger factors that secretly stimulate hidden pleasure centres in the brain. Only humans have this power to induce mental ecstasy and it can be triggered by hyper-arousal during group rituals. At times like this our brains are designed to freeload on the behavioural reward that encourages us to reproduce but without the physical involvement*".

Lomas explained that he was not saying that the ceremony gives rise to erotic feelings but that the same pleasure areas of the brain are stimulated as when experiencing an orgasm. He draws upon research that demonstrates that women who have had spinal injuries leaving them without feeling in the lower half of their bodies can still experience orgasm by genital stimulation and sees this being relevant to the pleasurable feelings masons get from the ritual. He seems to see sexual connotations in almost everything Masonic from the V shape of the Masonic square apparently represent the female pubic region to even the squared pavement and triangular pattern of borders around tracing boards as representing the uterus and eggs. He finds that these shapes evoke pleasurable feelings in the men taking part in the ritual. Lomas knew that something strange happens in the ritual but it seems to the author that he is barking up the wrong tree when he asks *"Are they (the Masonic rituals) just a sophisticated development of an insect mating ritual, modified for a species with a slightly larger bran?"*

In his 2005 lecture, "The Psychology of Freemasonry" to the Cornerstone Society, another Masonic research group, Kai Hughes admits that the ritual contains "tricks". He says *"ritual is another important element in creating a spiritual Lodge. It is through the delivery of the ritual that the spiritual story is told and, more importantly, experienced. There are a large number of 'tricks' that enable us to do this. If you want to know more about these 'tricks' read Robert Lomas' "Turning the Hiram key" in which he describes at great length his experience when he was initiated into freemasonry. However, whilst Lomas talks about the standard techniques for raising awareness such as putting the candidate into an ante room, blindfolding them to disorientate them, the element of surprise when the blind fold is removed, blood curdling threats etc etc, he fails to fully understand what the key purpose and deeper meaning of the ritual is".*

There seems to be some agreement that psychological "tricks" are employed in the ritual. Whereas Lomas believes they are there for increased cerebral pleasure and Hughes feels they are used in order that the candidate has a more spiritual experience, I believe that these techniques are cleverly obscured in the ritual by having apparently plausible explanations for them in terms of historical or mythical connotations and that they are actually there solely as a means of subconsciously influencing the candidate to behave in a predictable way going forward.

14) The Prisoner!

When I resigned from my Lodge, I was summoned to the Provincial 'Head Office' to explain why I had resigned. The interrogation lasted many hours and I was repeatedly asked why I had resigned, the panel not listening to or accepting my reasons. They probably knew that I was not sharing the real reason and I feared that if I did tell them, then they may be able to regain control over the situation and I would not be able to 'escape'.

Even after I was let go, I found that I was still bound to the organisation and every time I tried talking to others about my experiences something invisible reined me in and preventing me from talking about it.

In 1967, Patrick McGoohan delivered, through the medium of television, his allegorical story of 'The Prisoner'. Thirty years on, people are still debating the meaning of the series, numerous books and magazines have been published, there are societies for devoted fans and a growing number of web sites containing Prisoner images, sound clips, texts and theories. Here is an alternative and slightly less than serious review of 'The Prisoner' story as it might relate to Freemasonry.

The story starts with McGoonan's character resigning from his position within the secret service. The character is abducted and placed in the "Village" and assigned a number (Number Six). The hierarchy are determined to discover what he found out that caused him to resign. He rebels against all efforts to make him conform to village life and he continually attempts to escape.

Most episodes feature a different Number Two each time, whose task is to discover why Number Six resigned and why he challenged the authorities. If they can find out what Number Six discovered, they can bring him back into line - "if he will answer one simple question, the rest will follow. Why did he resign?"

The village is a beautiful place that has been around for "a long time" with everything bright and cheerful but where no citizen is free to leave. There is uniformity to their clothes and their language. Everyone is known as a number. The rules of the village are learned through signs placed around the village with messages such as "A still tongue makes a happy life", "Questions are a burden to others", "Of the people. By the people. For the people" and with those in power, and the villagers themselves, constantly repeating these slogans to each other.

Community loyalty is forced upon the villagers by an external force that decides what is best for them. They have been signed up "to care for each other and to see that the rules are obeyed". "Education", learning to conform, is accepted without a murmur. Music and important messages are communicated through loudspeakers on every corner. The village is controlled by an elusive Number One.

As well as these methods of control, the villagers are threatened with a gruesome punishment should they display an act of defiance. A mysterious white balloon appears at the immediate request of the village governors and the villagers freeze when commanded to. Should there be a defiant villager, the balloon will move towards him and suffocate him. The citizen will awaken in the care of the governors, questioned and after reconditioning, put back into the village.

Attempts are made to get Number Six to take up office but

he refuses to comply with the system that operates the village. "I am not a number, I am a person", "I've resigned. My life is my own". Number Two's duty is to see that he does comply - "you must conform! It is my sworn duty to see that you do conform". Number Six declares that he intends to escape and come back to destroy the village. Eventually, Number Two orders the ultimate method for bringing non-conformists under control - the "Degree Absolute", a test that will result in death for one of the participants. In the end, the odd man out beats them at their own game and succeeds in escaping from the village.

There are many theories as to the meaning of The Prisoner. Some suggest that the message is about the nature of freedom and the raising of the television viewer's consciousness. Others believe it to be a prophetic warning about the dangers of New Labour and social control.

To me, The Prisoner reminded me of my own experiences and I pondered whether the 'secret service' that McGoohan was trying to escape from might well have been Freemasonry and was he using the allegory of the spy story to describe his personal battle to regain his free will?

15) Summary & Conclusion

Members of the public are aware that Freemasonry has something to do with charity but it is mainly known for its secrecy. Masons rarely declare their membership openly and would certainly never disclose any of what happens at their meetings (even those who have left the order). They will claim that they are not a secret society but a "private society with some secrets" that promotes high moral values and donates large sums to charity.

The question the public have been asking for centuries is "If there is nothing sinister about Freemasonry, why the secrecy?" and up till now they haven't received a satisfactory answer. Those joining Freemasonry are also at first interested in answering this question but they soon become so involved with Freemasonry that they stop analysing their situation objectively. Those that do join only in order to find out what's going on and resist getting drawn fully into Freemasonry, soon get bored and leave, deciding that the whole thing is mumbo-jumbo and a waste of their valuable time.

There have been many exposures of the Masonic ritual in the past which in themselves have not answered any real questions. In fact they have further confused the issue, since any member of the public that can stay awake long enough to read through the ritual of the three degrees will conclude that it is nothing more than the script to a very boring play about moral principles and will still be left with the question "Why the secrecy?".

Most Masons get drawn into Freemasonry through their friends, family or business colleagues with the unspoken promise of social and/or business advancement. There are a small minority of unscrupulous individuals that will connive to use the cover of Freemasonry and its organisational structure for their own ulterior motives and when exposed, these are the stories that get into the press and give Freemasonry its bad name. There are, however, many hundreds of thousands of Masons, who quietly attend Lodge meetings when summoned, who have never been involved in any scandals or wrong doings.

The process starts a long time before a Mason is initiated. As part of the recruitment process, which is itself, effectively, part of the ritual and can take up to a year, he is subtly manipulated so that on the day of his initiation, he steadily perseveres through the ceremony without questioning or challenging any of the things that happen to him.

The ceremony itself cleverly masks, so that even those conducting it are completely unaware, that a powerful process of hypnotic induction is taking place. This culminates in the new candidate readily accepting that he entered Freemasonry and took the Masonic Oath of his own free will and accord. This ruse is similar in concept to the induction ploys that Stage Hypnotists use to hook their subjects into a false belief. Once this first step has been taken, the rest is easy. The rest of the initiation ceremony establishes the authority of senior members over the new recruit, a commitment to giving to Masonic charities, the suggestion that he will learn the true secrets of nature and mysteries of the universe and above all else, the fear that should he ever reveal anything about Freemasonry, the most gruesome of penalties will befall him, if not in this life, then the next.

Those innocently conducting the ritual, who are mainly concerned that they appear to be delivering a good performance, and those passively watching from the sidelines, are also having these powerful suggestions constantly reinforced. The other ceremonies (degrees) that the candidate undergoes further bond him in with particularly dramatic and, for some, frightening, experiences in the 3rd degree that finally "make" him a Master Mason.

From then on in, he is part of the unquestioning establishment looking for new recruits and gradually takes on more responsibility for processing them by moving up through the ranks eventually to become Master of the Lodge for a year and thereafter a Past Master. Thus, the ritual is simply about processing new members and by either active or passive involvement constantly reinforcing the hypnotic suggestions that were instilled into the existing members when they were first initiated.

Behaviourists, such as Skinner, have shown that behaviour and beliefs, regularly reinforced with promises of reward or fear of punishment, can be permanently established.

W. Kirk MacNaulty, writing in "Freemasonry, a Journey through Ritual and Symbol", 1991, comments that the origins of Freemasonry are intentionally obscure. One view is that the hierarchy purposely allows the publication of fanciful theories purporting to reveal the "true" origins of Freemasonry which include the builders of pyramids, the Knights Templar and the medieval guilds of stonemasons, since the more ancient and mysterious the past, the easier it is to make Masons believe that they are part of something special and holders of some secret esoteric knowledge. They are taught that this knowledge is in a coded form and that although they themselves are unable to unravel it, it is their duty to preserve it and pass it on to following generations in a manner somewhat similar to the characters in Umberto Eco's "Foucault's Pendulum".

The point has been illustrated in this work, that groups and organisations founded by a few committed individuals with a common cause, are often "hijacked" by another body that use the organisation of the original group as a vehicle for their own political or criminal ends. Could this be what happened to Freemasonry when the Grand Lodge was set up by apparently gathering together four existing London lodges? Very little is recorded about the motivations behind this "take-over" or who the prime movers were. Even John Hamill, Grand Lodge Librarian, admits "*why the Grand Lodge came into existence in 1717 has never been answered satisfactorily*". What is known though, is that those individuals that formed the Grand Lodge took control over the other Lodges and introduced rules and regulations by which they governed and maintained their authority. The ritual was adapted and amended to suit their own purposes and an ancient history was invented, and as George Orwell in "Nineteen Eighty Four" (1954) pointed out, "*who controls the past controls the future: who controls the present controls the past*".

Rival Grand Lodges soon sprang up and became hooked on competing with each other for new members and building bigger and bigger organisations. After almost a hundred years of this competition, the two main rivals amalgamated in 1813 and created the United Grand Lodge of England, probably the worlds' largest organisation after organised religion.

Obviously such an organisation with branches all over the world would be very important politically and we see that on the one hand, the Catholic Church tried to stop its advance while on the other, English Royalty (Head of the Church of England) became very involved in the early days of Grand Lodge eventually becoming its leader and promoter, a position it still holds today in the person of the Duke of Kent, the Grand Master.

The early individual Lodges probably collected charity from

their members for the benefit of their local communities with similar motives to the founders of the Society of St. Vincent de Paul. With the formation of Grand Lodge, these charities became centrally organised with a requirement that the local Lodges contribute to these central charities. Vast sums were amassed, the administration of which was handled by committees comprised of handpicked members chosen personally by the Grand Master.

Individual Lodges also had to pay membership subscriptions to Grand Lodge and so the more member Lodges that were formed, the wealthier Grand Lodge became. In turn, the hierarchy enjoyed a more luxurious lifestyle with the Masonic nobility held in awe and swanning around their provinces virtually worshipped by their congregations.

Sociologists have shown that these types of organisational structures have a tendency to persist over time, long after they have served their initial purpose, by readjusting or redefining their goals and objectives. There seems to be an almost innate social mechanism at work that causes members of such groups to preserve the organisation at all costs. Perhaps this is rationalised based on a sense of duty to the founders, a need to maintain the social structure in which their participation provides meaningful reference points, a belief that the fundamental principles need to be upheld and out of loyalty to their colleagues who are also dependent upon the social structure. Arnold also points out that "*institutions have self-perpetuating lives that ignore the signs of decay long after these have become apparent to outsiders*".

The religious aspects of Freemasonry keep the ceremonies solemn and enable the less religious of men to feel that they have satisfied this fundamental social requirement. It arouses in many a spiritual attachment to Freemasonry which also helps to maintain the authority structure in the same way that it works in the Church, with the more senior members apparently more enlightened and "better" people.

Apart from the basic three degrees, there are numerous Masonic orders and organisations that a qualified mason can join all of which have joining fees and their own peculiar ceremonies and regalia which the Mason is required to purchase. Not surprisingly, there are very few establishments that sell the required paraphernalia. Such a business would be a goldmine, selling pieces of material, books and special jewellery at inflated prices to a captured and expanding market who were obliged to buy. The leading suppliers of such items are based just across the road from the headquarters of the United Grand Lodge of England and have been in business since 1685! These financial aspects have over the years attracted many unscrupulous operators who set up spurious Masonic orders in order to prey on gullible Masons.

Freemasonry appears to use cult-like techniques to indoctrinate new members and maintain a powerful hold over them. The effect is so strong that even those that leave feel unable to share their experiences with non-members. Guy Arnold explains "*the impact of brainwashing often outlasts belief in the original institution*". In fact, as pointed out earlier, people cannot leave the organisation voluntarily, they can only be expelled or invited to resign. The main task of the members is to recruit "suitable candidates" (which according to Arnold are likely to be "*willing or at least pliant victims, that provide exceptionally malleable material for brainwashing*") and to unwittingly take part in ceremonies that process the new members into like minded individuals. Whereas other cults use brute psychological force to ensnare people within the space of a few days, Freemasonry achieves this very gradually and subtly over a number of months and years.

Guy Arnold was unable to include Freemasonry in his book on brainwashing as he could not get access to the required information. After reviewing "Freemasonry Inside Out", Guy Arnold in a private letter to me confirmed *"The techniques used by the Freemasons, the secrecy, the hierarchical structures and, later, the employment of longer-serving Masons to exert pressures upon newcomers - are each examples of long-used and understood "brainwashing" techniques, measures designed to bind individuals to the service of the organisation, the greater whole. Such techniques have been used by organised religions over many centuries."*

In addition to the techniques, that Arnold describes as brainwashing, unknowingly used on Masons by Masons, they are also passing on from generation to generation, the knowledge, buried in the ritual, of how to induce a hypnotic trance in unsuspecting individuals that make them more susceptible to suggestions and easier to control. This seems to be the real link with the ancient mystery schools dating back to Egyptian times. As Darual comments, *"the real mystery of the mysteries is how and when man first discovered the use of certain procedures to condition other men."*

Whenever there has been a public outcry such as when a new book appears or corruption proved, the organisation responds by mounting a PR campaign or amending its rituals and appears to embrace openness. Author Dominic Torr refers to this as "Masonic glasnost". This is not done to satisfy the public outcry but because it noticed a dramatic fall in recruitment levels.

If Freemasonry were to yield to the public's demand to "come out of the closet" and dispense with its shroud of secrecy, it would have to dispense with that part of the ritual that dealt with secrecy. This in turn would expose the hidden mechanisms of control - the mortar that holds the organisation together. Almost certainly, there would be resignations, recruitment would virtually cease overnight and the Masonic Machine would rapidly grind to a halt. No wonder Freemasonry goes to such lengths to protect its "secrets" because like the conjurors trick, once one knows how it works, it doesn't work anymore.

So the big SECRET is that the experience of the ritual (rather than any printed text that anyone can read) which most Masons regard as harmless mumbo-jumbo that has to be endured prior to enjoying the convivial atmosphere of the after-ceremony meal, actually contains cleverly concealed and powerful psychological techniques that are effective even though the Masons do not really take much notice of them. These techniques are not only employed to bind the men into keeping the ritual secret from outsiders and lower ranks, but also prevents the men themselves from objectively analysing the ritual. This influence lasts long after a Mason leaves the fraternity, in most cases for as long as he lives. This impenetrable schema has endured for almost 300 years and it has taken a unique set of circumstances to unlock this door. If we accept that the foregoing establishes what the secret is and how it has been kept secret, we are still left with the question of why there is this secret and what is the point of it.

There are many theories about the raison d'être of Freemasonry with the more fanciful writers focussing on a world domination conspiracy through a New World Order - there is even a board game called Illuminati! Perhaps the answer is more down to earth. Every person who has had thoughts or ideas about Freemasonry, including the members themselves, have usually taken the issue of charity for granted and ignored it completely in connection with the more sensational aspects of secrecy and conspiracy.

During the 1600's the Crown was focused on raising money

through a variety of inventive taxes and other schemes including outright theft, mainly to fund its battles and wars and to reward its supporters. By the 1700's the relationship between the Crown and Parliament was very different with limited opportunities for the Crown to independently raise funds.

History shows us that neither the Crown nor government were interested in charity and relief of the poor, and this was left to religious groups and wealthy merchants. It was noted earlier that the merchants had raised over £1,000,000 which was a massive sum by 17th century standards. It is suggested that some of these men founded the early Masonic type lodges where merchants of different faiths could come together for mainly charitable purposes. They had to meet in secret because of the severe punishment associated with not conforming to the State religion.

Could a small group of aristocratic conspirators in the early 1700's, possibly backed by the Crown, have designed a scam to take advantage of the good nature of these wealthy merchants? Perhaps they set about setting up their own spurious charity and sought to divert the merchants' charitable donations into it for their own purposes. The scheme would have been designed to attract men based on religious freedoms and charitable works. The added spice of learning about the mystical would have provided the rationale for secrecy. Thus the Grand Lodge could have been set up in 1717 by utilising the existing secret Masonic structure as a cover and even adding 4000 years to the calendar to imply that it had been around since "time immemorial" which according to Lomas coincides with the development of Sumer, the first known civilisation.

By imbedding mind control techniques learned from earlier secret societies and cults into the ritual, it was adapted in order to bind men into the organisation and keep them focused on working for the Masonic charity and expanding the organisation through the recruitment and indoctrination of new members. The cleverly designed token reward system of Masonic honours, which in the main offered "past" offices (i.e. non-active and thus meaningless), further encouraged men to make large charitable donations and to recruit others and then to form new Lodges in much the same way as today's multi-level pyramid sales scams operate.

As the Parliamentary system developed, the Crown had less direct control over public servants and the like, and Freemasonry offered an opportunity to maintain this control and thus these types were recruited as well. Parliament was unable to halt its progress but it was able to stop Freemasonry in 1768 from becoming incorporated and thus limit its opportunity for misappropriating the charity funds it was building up.

In addition to the financial aspects, Freemasonry could have enabled the Crown to keep the wealthy and influential merchant class subservient to the monarchy through the Masonic allegiance. Furthermore, it could have also provided the Monarch with influence overseas through the international growth of the organisation and its underground communications network.

The Grand Lodge had a clear run for about 30 years before others figured out what was going on and set up their own alternative Grand Lodges. It is not surprising that they competed so vigorously for new recruits. In 1813, there was either a take-over or merger and the United Grand Lodge was formed.

Freemasonry still uses cult-like mind control techniques, refined over hundreds of years, to control its members, expand its operation and keep the charity coffers full. The "Masonic machine" generates millions of pounds every year in the name of charity and filters this up to the Grand Charity (which the reader will remember is "*not under*" the Grand Lodge). Other income is derived from investments (made by "speculative" masons) and the legacies of deceased Masons. Misappropriating the charity funds is more difficult these days with the controls of legislation, taxation and the Charity Commissioners. However questions are asked about whether the main beneficiaries of the subsidised retirement homes and private education funded by the membership as a whole are fairly spread across the membership or skewed towards a particular cross section and also how much money is consumed through "operating expenses".

Freemasonry has always stressed its charitable activities which were almost exclusively for the benefit of Freemasons and their families. But since the 'glasnost' campaign began in the 1980s major efforts have been made to publicise the substantial donations that Grand Lodge and individual lodges now make to non-Masonic charities. There is though, no way of assessing what percentage of Masonic charity now goes to outside organisations.

Freemasonry became a matter of considerable public and media interest in the 1980s after the John Stalker affair, where there was speculation that it was Masonic influence from within the police force that caused him to be removed from the Northern Ireland "shoot to kill" inquiry and with the publication of Stephen Knight's and Martin Short's books and Short's television series.

In 1995, as Prime Minister at that time, John Major was in favour of a requirement that public servants declare membership of Freemasonry and this was backed by Jack Straw, then shadow Home Secretary.

A House of Commons Select Committee on Home Affairs started to gather written evidence on the role Freemasonry plays in the lives of public servants such as police officers, judges, solicitors and barristers ("The Lawyer", 5/11/95) and was due to hold the inquiry in June 1996. Sir John Welch, a senior mason and client partner at law firm Wedlake Bell for Grand Lodge said at the time, "*if it's just a question of knocking an organisation that may be perceived to be part of the establishment, then I would object. If there is a valid reason for it, then the more investigations the better because hopefully the masons will come out of it unscathed*".

On the surface Freemasonry appeared to welcome the inquiry. John Hamill, Grand Lodge Librarian said at that time "*an examination based on facts will do much to dispel the myths*". But did Freemasonry really want the facts laid bare and the myths dispelled? The Observer reported in March 1996 under the headline "MPs stall probe into the Masons" there was much hostility within the Tory ranks to the inquiry and that it was hoped that it was unlikely to go ahead because of "more pressing business".

In the event though, the committee continued to collect written evidence and despite a change of Government in 1997, it proceeded to hold its inquiry.

Under the chairmanship of Labour MP Chris Mullin, the Committee continued the Conservative enquiry and after taking evidence, despite attempts by Grand Lodge Grand Secretary Higham to thwart the process and without any evidence submitted by declared Freemasons, the Committee published its reports into the influence of Freemasons on public life.

One of the key recommendations was that voluntary registers should be set up where Freemasons in public life, particularly people working in the criminal justice system should state whether they were Freemasons or not.

In May 1999, the BBC website ("UK Politics Call to Free Up Masons" 26 May 1999) reported that the Committee were very disappointed with the number that had complied. Chris Mullin said that voluntary registration of membership was failing due to "foot dragging" within some branches of the legal system and when asked if new laws were needed on disclosure he said "They'll have to be if anything is going to change".

Despite much support from Home Secretary Jack Straw, and even with the Committee watering down its recommendations in the hope of getting a higher percentage take up of voluntary registrations, the final blow was struck when Grand Lodge threatened to take the Government to Court using a European Court decision concerning the Italian precedent that some Masons' human rights were violated when the authorities tried to curb Masonic secrecy. This led Jack Straw to withdraw what was left of the requirements that the judiciary register membership in a House of Commons Statement in 2009. This effectively led to ending the attempt to oblige police and public prosecutors to register.

From this time forward, there has been a lack of interest in Freemasonry with politicians, the press, TV, publishers, etc., all avoiding "tangling" with Freemasonry. It is as if Freemasonry has become an "unsubject" (see Nick Cohen's "You Can't Read This Book: Censorship in an Age of Freedom", 2012 – and even he won't touch Freemasonry!).

In 2012, a body called the Social Issues Research Centre (SIRC) published an "independent" and "objective" report entitled "The Future of Freemasonry". According to Freemasonry Today (March 2012), the reports "*highlights the importance that Freemasonry places on charitable giving, the part that many Freemasons play in their local communities and the central role of the family. As well as instilling in its members a moral and ethical approach to life – including thoughtfulness for others, kindness in the community, honesty in business, courtesy in society and fairness in all things – Freemasons are the largest charitable givers after the National Lottery, and also make major contributions to international disaster relief funds."* There is a very close relationship between the SIRC and MCM Research Ltd, a PR company for businesses with an image problem and is notable for its many alcohol industry clients. MCM partly funds the SIRC and the SIRC publishes reports produced by the MCM. Perhaps for this reason, when the Grand Secretary made much of presenting this report, the media hardly noticed.

It would seem that Grand Lodge has succeeded with its "glasnost" campaign using the dual methods of spreading the image of a benign charitable brotherhood, impeccable because headed by Royalty, busy making good men better and no threat to anyone - while simultaneously instilling fear not only in the media but in the Government itself.

The media and the general public assume, because of the lack of media attention, that Freemasonry is out of step with the times and is withering away. Although young men these days do not tend to follow their fathers into Freemasonry as they did in the past, it is still vital for the organisation to recruit new blood. To this end, a special focus has been placed on trying to recruit university students and staff as reported in The Education Guardian (8 June 2007) under the headline "Freemasons begin university recruitment drive". It states that *"The English masonic lodge is looking to boost its numbers by actively recruiting students and staff from several UK universities."* It goes on to say that nine specific universities have been targeted, namely Bath, Birmingham, Bristol,

Cambridge, Durham, Exeter, Manchester, Oxford and Sheffield, but the aim is to gradually expand it beyond these universities. There is even an innocuous sounding website, www.universitiesscheme.com which is a recruiting ground for students and university staff with the ultimate aim of establishing university lodges.

While the 'old fashioned' country gentleman style Freemasonry (based on genuine brotherhood values) appears to be eroding and where previously one had to ask an existing Freemason they knew personally about joining, there is now a focussed campaign to recruit the influencers and leaders of tomorrow among the student population. Meanwhile, although numbers overall are diminishing, recruitment of new members in the 30 to 50 age range in the key professions of the law, finance and the media remains as dynamic as ever.

So Freemasonry remains still today a very real, and in some case questionable, presence in our society and - with some 5 million members claimed worldwide solely for Grand Lodges recognised by UGLE - in the world as a whole. And this entire movement is held together and influenced by secret, subtle but powerful, psychological processes.

I have written this book because I believe that the general public and the individuals within it, should in their own interest be far better informed about Freemasonry after the media's near two decades of imposed silence.

There are many positives in the form of Charity and Brotherly Love (two of the three great pillars of Freemasonry that have helped keep the organisation together for over 300 years) but it is the free will myth that concerns me the most and as things stand. Truth, apparently the greatest of the Masonic virtues, could yet prove to be the final nail in Hiram Abiff's coffin.

References

Arnold, Guy. *Brainwash: The Cover-up Society*, 1992

Baigent & Leigh, *The Temple and the Lodge*, 1989

Baigent, Leigh & Lincoln. *The Holy Blood and the Holy Grail*, 1982

Bowler, J E. *Masons Marks in Cyprus*, 1938

Briggs, Asa. *A Social History of England*, 1983

Brooke, John. *King George III*, 1972

Cohen, Nick. *You Can't Read This Book,* 2012

Crowe, Fred. *The Master Masons Hand Book*, 1894

Crush, Peter. *A Very Grand Secretary*, in Human Resources Magazine, August 2001

Daraul, Arkon. *Secret Societies*, 1961

Denslow, William R. *10,000 Famous Freemasons,* 1957-60

Doyle, Sir Arthur Conan. *Early Psychic Experiences*, 1924

Feynman, Richard. *Surely you're joking Mr Feynman*, 1985

Gilbert, R.A. *The Golden Dawn Companion*, 1986

Gilbert, R.A. *The Magical Mason*, 1983

Glen, Frederick. *The Social Psychology of Organizations*, 1975

Greenberg, Ira. *Group Hypnotherapy and Hypnodrama*, 1977

Grinder and Bandler, *TRANCE-formations: Neuro- Linguistic Programming*, 1981

Hall, Manly. *The Freemasonry of the Ancient Egyptians*, 1982

Hamill, John. *Ancient Wisdom and Secret Sects*, 1989

Hamill, John. *The Craft: A History of English Freemasonry*, 1986

Hannah, Walton. *Darkness Visible*, 1952

Hill, Christopher. *The Century of Revolution 1603 - 1714*, 1980

Hounam, Peter and Hogg, Andrew. *Secret Cult*, 1984

Inglis, Brian. *TRANCE - A Natural History of Altered States of Mind*, 1989

Knight, Charles. *Old England: A Pictorial Museum*, originally published in 1847

Knight, Christopher & Lomas, Robert. *The Hiram Key*, 1996

Knight, Stephen. *The Brotherhood*, 1984

Laake, Deborah. *Secret Ceremonies, A Mormon Woman's Intimate Diary*, 1993

Le Bon, Gustave. *The Crowd: A Study of the Popular Mind*, 1896

Le Forestier, Rene. *Templar and Occult Freemasonry*, 1970

Leadbeater, C W. *The Hidden Life in Freemasonry*, 1926

Luck, Georg. *Arcana Mundi*, 1985

Lutyens, Mary. *J.Krishnamurti: The Years of Fulfilment*, 1983

Macionis, John. *Sociology*, 1989

MacNaulty, W. Kirk. *Freemasonry - A Journey through Ritual & Symbol*, 1991.

Magus Incognito, *The Secret Doctrine of the Rosicrucians*, 1949

Paine, Thomas. *The Age of Reason*, 1973

Rachlin, Howard. *Introduction to Modern Behaviourism*, 1970

Robinson, John. *Born in Blood - The Lost Secrets of Freemasonry*, 1989

Roth, Cecil. *A History of the Jews in England*, 1964

Schonfield, Hugh. *The Essene Odyssey*, 1993

Schwaller de Lubicz, R A. *Esoterism & Symbol*, 1985

Schwaller de Lubicz, R A. *The Temple in Man: Sacred Architecture and the Perfect Man*

Short, Martin. *Inside the Brotherhood*, 1989

Society of St. Vincent de Paul. *The Manual*, 1958

Stalker, John. *Stalker*, 1988

Stewart, Trevor. in Hutchinson's *The Spirit of Masonry*, 1775, (1987 edition)

Storm, Rachel. *In Search of Heaven on Earth*, 1991

Temple, Robert. *Open to Suggestion - The Uses and Abuses of Hypnosis*, 1989

Tolstoy. *War and Peace*, 1868

Torr, Dominic. *Hoodwink*. 2011

Vibert, Lionel. *The Rare Books of Freemasonry*, 1987

Wilmshurst, W. L. *The Meaning of Masonry*, 1927

Wolpert, Lewis. *Literary Review*, April 1993